THE YEAR OF LIVING MAGICALLY:

PRACTICAL WAYS TO CREATE A LIFE OF SPIRIT, WONDER AND CONNECTION

BY

PAUL J. LESLIE

OTHER BOOKS BY PAUL J. LESLIE

LOW COUNTRY SHAMANISM: AN EXPLORATION OF THE MAGICAL AND HEALING PRACTICES OF THE COASTAL CAROLINAS AND GEORGIA

POTENTIAL NOT PATHOLOGY: HELPING YOUR CLIENTS TRANSFORM USING ERICKSONAIN PSYCHOTHERAPY

GET OUT OF YOUR SEAT: AN AVERAGE PASSENGER'S GUIDE TO OVERCOMING AIRLINE TERROR (WITH IAN COX)

TABLE OF CONTENTS

ACKNOWLEDGMENTS

I want to acknowledge those whose help have made this work possible:

Catherine Carrigan and RamaJon, whose assistance and direction were crucial in getting this work to publication,

Frank Lorcha and Thomas Abernathy, who always reminded me to laugh, even at times when I didn't think I could,

My parents, Paul and Sue Leslie, who continue to be my greatest source of love, encouragement and support (special thanks to Sue, whose editorial insights and suggestions were immensely helpful).

INTRODUCTION

"What do you think Paul?"

The comment woke me up from my trance of observing clouds drift by in the sky. "I'm not sure," I said to cover for my lack of attention.

"Same here," said one of my colleagues sitting behind me.

I was in a large classroom at the college where I worked. I was part of a committee to implement a program focusing on critical thinking throughout all the courses taught at the college. It was a very daunting task because of the sheer number of courses taught and because we also had to rewrite nearly every assignment to ensure that a specific model of critical thinking was implemented.

As I regained my awareness of what was transpiring in the meeting, the head of the committee, Debra, looked at me and said, "You don't seem much like yourself today." I smiled and told her that I didn't feel much like myself today. She smiled and continued with focusing our attention on yet another mind numbing class assignment needing adjustments in order to reflect critical thinking competencies. I began to ask myself, "Is this really my life now?' The past year had been one of the most difficult of my life and having to do mindless committee work did little to inspire me.

A year earlier my wife of several years decided that she could no longer take the arguing and disagreements that emanated from our home. She had been unhappy for a long time. It seemed that nothing I did ever made her happy, and she was often angry with me about things which often did not even involve me. I tried as hard as I could not to get upset, but it became a daily emotional battle which my introverted nature could barely tolerate. After one truly heated exchange of anger between us, my wife told me she was done with our relationship. I begged and pleaded for her to stay. I was willing to do anything, within reason, to make the marriage work. She did not relent. She had made up her mind and had cut me out of her life in what I perceived as a very cold manner.

I was wounded beyond belief. I had never experienced such emotional devastation. I felt I had put everything I had into the relationship, mentally, physically, financially and emotionally. Due to the emotional volatility between us, I decided to move out for a while leaving my wife and her daughter, both of whom I loved very much, in the house. I was hoping things would eventually calm down without me around to light another emotional powder keg. I also needed to leave for my own sanity. Being ignored and then lashed out at from the woman I deeply loved was much too painful for me. I moved into a small furnished one bedroom apartment at the top of a three story one hundred year old house with little to no insulation. These conditions made the winter bitterly cold and the summer heat downright unbearable. As I sat alone in this old, uncomfortable apartment I replayed in my mind where things had gone wrong in my marriage and what I thought I should have done to have saved it.

Eventually, my wife moved out of the house and I was able to move back in. With a renewed love of central heating and air, I attempted to get my life back to normal although I had no idea what normal was. I not only had to learn to live without my wife and stepdaughter, which was painful enough, but I also needed to figure out where to go in my own life. I was overwhelmed, without direction, and completely confused. My best laid plans had fallen apart and I had no clue as to what I was really supposed to be doing in my life. As I sat in the college committee meeting, I began to really think about my life. That very same morning I had sat in my car in the driveway of my home wondering if this is all that there was for me. Surely I was being rather ungrateful feeling this discontent. I had become what many people would consider "successful". I had a good job teaching psychology at the local community college. I had a thriving psychotherapy practice where I saw and helped many clients. I had published well received books which had given me some national and regional exposure. I had presented at conferences and published articles in peer reviewed journals. I had a very nice home in a very nice neighborhood. I was, by many standards, "living the dream", but all I felt as I sat in the driveway that morning was emptiness and confusion.

I had succeeded more than I expected but yet I was not happy. It was not just the failed marriage. Something was missing and I couldn't quite put my finger on it. I had wanted to accomplish certain goals but when I pursued them and succeeded, there was little gratification. To be honest, I felt I was just completing one mindless goal and then moving onto the next mindless goal. I was drifting without any direction, like a ghost ship on the open sea, still moving with the tides but vacant and lifeless none the less.

At the end of a long week I settled into the weekend with a nagging feeling of existential angst. I sat in my favorite chair and just quietly listened to the sounds of emptiness in the house. The house, devoid of family noises, sat quiet and lonely. The only sounds were an occasional car driving by in the neighborhood and the sound of my own breath. I was truly alone. Life held very few positive feelings at the moment. I wanted to curl up and die. I had hit a low level of depression which I had been fighting against the past year. I was hurt, angry and in despair. Rationally, I knew that things would eventually improve but emotionally I couldn't see any future in the moment. It was another lonely night in a meaningless world for me.

That night I came across a book I had previously read several years earlier, but at that time it had not made much of an impact. The book was "The Re-enchantment of Every Day Life" by Thomas Moore. Moore, who had had been a monk and a psychotherapist, wrote several well received books on spirituality and depth psychology. In this particular book, he passionately implored people to find spirit in their lives through interactions with the natural earth. He believed these interactions welcome mystery and magic. Approaching the world this way was in contrast to a strict detached scientific perspective. He argued that much of our enjoyment of being alive can be found in making the everyday world more magical and soulful. When we move away from interacting with the natural earth as a living, magical place we find ourselves lifeless and empty.

As I read this book again something in me started to wake up. I realized that I had absolutely no magic in my life. Life had become dull and lifeless just as Moore described. The daily routine was that I worked, worked, and then worked some more only to then sometimes sleep. The natural world around me was an afterthought instead of an amazing living system filled with mystery. I had become a left brained linear thinker who had lost his connection to his creative self. In essence, I was going through the motions of existing instead of living a magical life. Intuitively I knew that something was not right as I continued to run on the professional treadmill. My life had become devoid of mystery and sacredness.

These ideas were a little difficult for me to initially accept because I had become a "realist", viewing the world through the lens of an existential agnostic. The firing of neurons and distribution of chemicals in the brain were the only factors that made us who we are. Somewhere the sense of wonder had been lost, a victim of the strict materialistic views which I taught in my psychology courses at the college. Logic had been embraced to a point where my creative mind had to take a backseat. Having logic in one's life can be very helpful, but I had let it overtake me to the point that the mysterious and the magical were qualities which I had problems accessing.

I began to wonder if the lack of magic in my life was related to my ongoing discontent with the world itself. I never seemed to be satisfied with anything the world presented me. My achievements were nice, but I always seemed to be on the lookout for something else, never giving myself time to truly appreciate what I had. My goal oriented mindset, which admittedly had given me professional success, stood in the way to living an enchanted existence. If my time on Earth was to be mostly spent on achieving a constant stream of goals which did not really make me happy, then what did it all matter anyway? If I was not happy chasing unfulfilling things, then why not stop the chase? Clearly this was a mental, emotional and spiritual crossroads in my life.

Reflecting on Moore's encouragement to seek out enchantment in their lives, I decided to apply my goal directed nature toward a new goal, which was different from any I had previously pursued. I decided to live a magical life for the next year. I wanted to balance my left brained logical thinking with my right brained intuitive magical side. This may sound easy but it proved to be more difficult than anticipated. I had become hardwired to immediately dismiss anything which did not automatically conform to my preconceived ideas as to what was considered logical. I initially struggled to transform my own thoughts, which had become well-conditioned naysayers to anything magical. I desired a new openness to the world around me. This new approach confounded my left brain nature, but I tried to give my creative right brain as much room to roam as possible.

When I began to explore life as a magical experience, I

researched what specifically is "a magical life." The opinions were varied as I read such diverse topics as philosophy, depth psychology, mythology, mysticism and theology. I found many people who self-styled themselves as "magicians", dabbled in the Western Occult traditions (Occult meaning "secret"), and talked pretty big but had little to show for all of their self-proclaimed spiritual power. I had to maneuver through many ridiculous claims and nonsense that just didn't sound much like a magical life at all.

Eventually I determined that a magical life is not about obtaining great power to direct the Universe to your bidding or becoming a self-proclaimed wizard who asserts he can conjure demons from the astral plane. Rather, the magical life is learning to live with the natural ebb and flow of nature in ways which brings great meaning and purpose to one's life. As we explore our world through a magical lens, we find that the mundane can become magical if we shift our perceptions. A magical life consists of being able to live our lives according to our own priorities by focusing our thoughts, words and actions on what is truly important to us. When we allow ourselves to explore our inner world and connect with the great mystery of our being, we experience a shift in what it means to be alive and what real success truly is to us. By opening up to the great myths of magical transformation history has given us, we can find ways to live our lives in contentment and passion in the present while gaining more peace and harmony in the things we do.

I wrote this book not just as a chronicle of my own inner journey toward living a magical life but as a way to

12

share with others the ideas and concepts which can stimulate their own creativity and initiate a balanced integration of left brained logic and right brained wisdom. The year I spent learning about opening up to a sense of the mysterious aided my becoming better at most everything I did. I became a better teacher and a better psychotherapist. By encouraging my students and clients to begin accessing their own inner realms for direction, they discovered new, empowering ways to direct their lives. I watched them grow in many surprising and remarkable ways which motivated me to further explore what it means to live a magical life.

In this book I have noted some of my own journey, but are also ideas and activities for those who may wish to begin living their lives in new and magical ways. I wanted to provide a simple path for others who desire to open up to the mysteries of life without losing their ability to be grounded critical thinkers. Too often people who decided to follow a spiritual path ultimately ended up flying off to the land of pure absurdity which only added to their existential angst. By having one foot planted in the world of magic and mystery we open ourselves up to many miraculous events but, we also need to keep our other foot firmly planted in the world of logic in order to balance our perceptions and avoid becoming gullible flakes. By creating a balance of magic and reason we have the best of both worlds and life becomes increasingly more interesting.

Living a magical life will look differently for each person so don't compare yourself to others. The magical life of the "type A" business person may look very different from that of the laid back pottery maker. Every person has her own path to follow, and the freedom to follow a path of one's own is crucial for magical living. In order to have magic in your life you must allow yourself to take your own path and allow more of your true self to emerge. For many people this can be a frightening scenario due to how our society often causes us to believe that it is not good enough to just be whom we are.

The first step to living a magical life is to be open to living differently. Even if the outer trappings of your life don't shift much, you will find that your inner world will become more rich and comforting. The more you connect deeply with yourself, the more you access resources which you did not know you had. Life will feel less burdensome and more fulfilling when you are open to an alternate view of life. Allow yourself to play and become curious as to what you will discover as you now begin your own magical journey.

CHAPTER 1: BEGINNING THE MAGICAL JOURNEY

In today's world we often find ourselves pursuing a life which purports to have great fulfillment yet leads to further depths of discontent. The unrelenting goal of pursuing and acquiring more and more things clouds our view of the world as a sacred place where life develops in the most amazing ways. In our culture, our hopes and dreams are regularly measured by the number of items we collect. In our pursuit of success, we juggle multiple areas of life ranging from business to personal in the hope that if our ability to juggle is effective then we can have it all. Unfortunately, for many people, there are too many balls in the air at one time. They have no inner feeling of competence and achievement.

In this difficult world of strictly material pursuits, we can never truly be centered. We live in a digital age where we are available twenty-four hours a day due to new technology which was supposed to make our lives easier. The constant cell phone and internet interactions further move us away from a true connection to others and the world around us. It seems that we are "on" all the time which adds to the demands of an already stressful life.

We also may find that our days are filled with activities which we truly do not enjoy. Many people find their days packed with outside expectations and obligations which do not excite, fulfill or nurture them. These perceived obligations are added into the already numerous activities and actions needed to be juggled on a daily basis.

The truth is that we live in an age of anxiety and depression. People are desperate to find inner direction amid the constant glaring push of technological advancement. People want to live more rewarding lives yet seem unable to break free of their views of this world as hostile and without purpose. Dichotomous lines have been drawn in the sand between spiritual and material views of our existence which keep us from realizing our true directions in life. More than anything, people want to have a significant existence in the short period in which they inhabit this earth.

In order to move past our endless obligations and expectations we operate under, it is important to actively make a change. Each of us has to decide that the outside world of chasing strictly material success is not the only focus of our lives. We each must decide that our inner world needs as much nurturing (if not more) as our outer world. We have to decide that the world of the physical, while important, is unbalanced if we do not pay attention to the realm of the spirit. If we want to live a magical life, it is up to us to make a life of spirited living a priority. There will always be goals in the material realm we need to accomplish. However, if we do not make a conscious effort to pay attention to our inner world, we may find that our attention will always be distracted by other events, people and situations which have little to add to the overall quality of our lives. It has been said that nature abhors a vacuum, and this can be seen whenever you allow any space in your life. If you don't make an effort to fill that space in your life for inner exploration, then nature has a way of filling it with something else (usually with something that does not inspire you).

I found that much of my life was spent feeling rather insignificant. Many of the goals I pursued were to give me a feeling of significance. Seeing my place in the world as inconsequential, I unconsciously began to believe I had to do greater and greater things to be significant. My belief system was viewed me and the world around me as an accident with no real importance. I found myself feeling a nagging sense of discontent and despair that would not go away no matter what goals I achieved. It was a recipe for stress and overworking. I sometimes felt like a hamster on a wheel, believing that if I just went a little faster, good things would happen. Sometimes they did, and sometimes they didn't. In the end, I was still running on the wheel with no clue as to how to get off.

One day I just decided that, if I was going to struggle in life, then I might as well enjoy the struggle as much as possible. I wondered how I could adjust my present life of monotony to a life of inspiration without having to change much in the outer world. I enjoyed many aspects of my life, but there was a nagging feeling of emptiness. Things had to change in my inside world before they could change in my outside world. At that moment I began a solitary quest for the next year. I was to discover how to bring more magic into the mundane. I desired to experience life without the constant feeling that I was not enough, did not have enough, and was not doing enough. Like one of King Arthur's knights, I metaphorically charged into the wasteland to find the Grail, which for me was a sense of mystery and wonder in life.

As the quest began to live a year of my life magically, I realized that many of my basic assumptions about the world would have to change or at least be suspended for a while. I needed to open up to possibilities which may have previously been dismissed out right. I began my journey with some trepidation. I wanted to feel a stronger connection to the magical, spiritual elements of life, but I was worried that I may become too open minded. Perhaps I would begin to believe in things far from any grounding in reality.

During early explorations of what it means to live magically, I read a good bit of work by philosophers from the Greek and Hellenic periods. Many of these individuals of wisdom were very much grounded in the practical, material world but yet also believed there was more to our existence than what our five senses tell. They possessed both a rigorous attitude for empiricism but also were open to the unseen forces which operate in our world. In studying these great thinkers, I found a definition of living in a magical society that was acceptable to me.

A society which embraces magical living will understand that mystery and wisdom often go hand in hand. Being able to live in the worlds of both materialism and imagination can often be difficult. Our culture demands that all experiences be dissected and then dismissed if they do not adhere to a materialistic world view. Our culture has difficulty being able to think outside of dichotomies. We see this in everything from sports teams to political parties. People who do not fit into a culturally agreed upon category have trouble connecting with others locked in rigid views about life. Building a tribe which consists of an "us against them" mentality may have short term gain, but in the long term, it lacks resources to make the world a better place.

It is by opening our minds to different views that allows us to embrace a magical way of life. We can see things through the lens of the material and imagination if we free ourselves from knee jerk conditioned responses. When we live at the deepest levels of mystery and magic, we open ourselves up to unseen realms of the unconscious mind guiding us into surprising areas of inner vision. This inner vision does not have to exclude the outer material realm. At the same time, we do not have to shut out any out of the ordinary feelings and experiences which cannot strictly be measured in a sterile laboratory setting. Living magically occurs when we allow spiritual influences to be brought into our consciousness while still being firmly rooted in the material world.

Many spiritual systems often have as their goal the transcending of the material world by pursuing a level of consciousness beyond earthly existence. This, in my opinion, is far different from consciously choosing to live a magical life. To live magically, I believe we can honor our spiritual side while also fully living in the material, sensory based world. Living magically, we can experience the joys of day to day life, but we also need to connect back with the source of our creativity and inspiration.

If one wants to experience a magical existence, it is so important to have a balance in both the spiritual and the material. Only giving credence to sensory driven, empirical data, we become cold and disconnected from our natural world. We will find little to no enchantment in our daily lives. In a world in which material possessions are so much more valued than spiritual and psychological development, it is easy to see examples of what happens when our spiritual side is devalued and scorned as we grow more inhumane to ourselves and others in a quest to dominate our environment.

At the same time, by being overly focused on esoteric and spiritual ideas, we run the risk of being ungrounded and prone to ridiculous flights of fantasy and unfounded new age conjectures. Examples of harmful cult behavior emanate from environments in which little common sense or critical thinking is exhibited. The desire to become special by only focusing on spiritual matters can rob one of the ability to think for oneself. There are enough horror stories of those who go looking for spiritual guidance only to be taken advantage of by charismatic gurus who chastise their followers for having any connection to the material world while the gurus take in vast amounts of material wealth from those they claim to be able to save. When people feel insignificant, they will do just about anything to gain some sense of being special even engaging in the most harmful and ridiculous activities.

When we have a firm grounding in the material world of objective thought along with a spiritual connection to the ebb and flow of nature, we are in a much better position to pursue material goals while feeling significant in just being who we are. We do not run out to the first snake oil salesman who, for a small fee, promises us a life without any discomfort. Nor do we ignore unexplained phenomena we experience which makes us feel connected to something greater than ourselves. By being grounded in both material and spiritual, we are in a position to interact and experience our lives with many possibilities.

"To have a stature great enough to raise its head to heaven and still keep its feet upon the earth is the proof of true enlightenment" – **Manly Hall**

As I began researching what it means to have a magical life, several consistent ideas seemed to appeared. I found that there several basic principles which regularly showed up when people began exploring the mysteries of our inner worlds. These principles appeared in such diverse areas as ancient philosophy, psychology and in my quiet talks with wise, older people whose opinions I value greatly. When I began incorporating these principles into my life, I noticed that I began to experience my world, which I had previously labeled as mundane, as a more alive and magical existence. I found that by making a subtle shift in how I saw my place in the universe. I was able to find a sense of significance and contentment which had been eluding me. By applying these principles, I began to enjoy my life more and relax. I was able to find a sense of purpose without losing my grounding in the everyday world. I used the information I found to balance my desires for my future with what was really important to me as a human being.

Now having written all that, I want to be clear that these principles are not a cure for every situation. You will still feel angry sometimes. You will still feel sad sometimes. You will still get your heartbroken sometimes. These are all a part of life. We can never really run away from our humanity. What these principles will give you is a way to live your life more in line with the flow of the natural world. As a result, you more than likely will experience less anger, less sadness and less heartbreak. But be realistic and know that all of these emotions exist to tell us something.

Each of these principles, these "magical life principles", is presented in everyday language with practical examples. I did not want anyone to have to wade through overwhelming technical jargon which may obscure these simple but profound concepts. Each principle also has exercises for you to complete. I highly encourage you to do each exercise. It will give you so much than a strict cerebral acknowledgement. It is usually experience which leads us to change, not mere reflection. Life is meant to be lived not just understood!

Magical life Principle #1 – Everything is Interconnected

Approaching the world magically is to explore the deep-rooted spirituality found in nature. It is in the interaction with nature which gives us the most central connection to spirit. Throughout history interaction with nature has been a catalyst for spiritual investigation by people of all cultures. Sterile discussions of nature pale in comparison to vivid, dynamic interactions with the living earth.

Active participation in the ebb and flow of nature give us an opportunity to create our experiences in life rather than fight against the inevitability of change. The rhythms of the natural world give us many lessons about how to approach our own lives. By utilizing the intelligence of nature we can view our lives with more meaning and purpose. This interconnection with nature's rhythms allows us to become more aware of our place in a larger community far beyond our limited views of self.

In ancient times people viewed their lives against the back drop of the four seasons in a cyclical pattern. Modern people see time as linear. In linear time there is no difference in one moment from another. There is no meaning or purpose beyond mechanical time keeping. In contrast, cyclical time was viewed holy days as days which coincide with harvest days or adjustments of the earth in equinoxes. Ancient people observed changes in the season as rhythmic sensations of a living universe rather than simply specific times on a calendar.

Today, many of us have minimal interactions with nature. Whereas our ancestors had a daily connection to the natural world, our interactions have become less and less. In the West, we live in a world where technical discoveries grasp our attention. As we continue to embrace more and more technical innovations, we also are minimizing and decreasing our connection with nature.

A part of all of us secretly longs for a connection to the deep mysteries of the natural world. This desire is often hidden behind out day to day accumulation of material things which, ultimately, add little value to our inner world. We spend more times indoors wired to a variety of devices than we spend outdoors experiencing nature first hand. I am not pushing an agenda to become completely free of technology. Far from it, but we do need bring equilibrium in our lives between technological achievements and naturalistic wonders. One does not have to give up all creature comforts and live off the land in order to have a magical life. It is by having stability in both worlds that opens us up to the wisdom of both the natural and material realms.

It is our connection with the Earth that we opens us to the sacred, whether we are devoutly religious or fiercely atheistic. When we reflect on the creative force of nature we find a systemic wisdom that provides us with the evidence that we do not exist in isolation. We are a part of a dynamic force that moves through everything. We open ourselves up to the realm of magical living when we both honor nature and ethically utilize its gifts to us.

As a child I was always drawn to playing in the woods near where I grew up. My friends and I would dig in the dirt and construct mock forts and clubhouses. We would climb trees and just sit in them for a long period of time. The woods seem to be alive with possibilities when I roamed them as a child. I felt a sense of connection to the woods. Today I see large numbers of young people who rarely go outside and are resistant to leaving their computers and video games. What passes as play now is far from the enjoyment out in the woods behind my home. Perhaps one of the reasons for the rise in anxiety and depression among our children is due to the lack of play in the natural world. Burning off excess energy running through the woods can also have long term health benefits in contrast to sitting for hours a day in excessive video game use.

When I began my journey to make life more magical, I decided it was time to go back into the woods and find my place in nature again. With a schedule as packed as mine, I had to carve out time and make going into the natural world a priority. Even if I only spent a few minutes a day outside I committed to being fully present during that time. Just sitting on the grass in my backyard for a few minutes could help me slow down and focus better. Lying on my back on the grass and looking up at the clouds helped me in feeling more grounded. Standing in the backyard at night and bathing in the glow of a full moon gave me a sense of peace at the end of a day which had been filled with emotional upheavals.

I found great joy in driving over to a state park located near my home where trails for hiking were in abundance. I enjoyed going when few people were present and was able to allow all my senses to fully experience the natural realm. I found solace sitting beside a creek which comforted me with its bubbling sounds and sparkling water. When fully present in that setting, I found many ideas and solutions to problems came forth easily. Watching birds soar overhead and ants work down below reinforced the systemic nature of our world.

A therapy client of mine, Josh, found that simply being outside in nature helped him to deal with his post-traumatic stress disorder. Josh had been in combat during the war in Iraq and came home feeling severely anxious and unable to focus on his daily life. Josh told me that what had been helpful to him was to go deer hunting. The truth was, according to Josh, he didn't really hunt deer at all. He took his rifle out and sat in a deer stand for several hours. He never shot a deer during this time. He just sat quietly in his deer stand and allowed the sights and sounds of nature to shift his mood. He said that it took about fifteen minutes in the deer stand to begin feeling a change. He noticed that his breathing slowed down and his jaw relaxed. He also noticed tightness which had been in his body a half hour previously, began to disappear. When he returned home from his hunt, his family noticed the difference in his mood. They found that for the rest of the day Josh was less irritable and anxious. His family encouraged him to go deer hunting more often even though he was not bringing home any deer. It was by his interacting with nature that Josh found a deep sense of peace which aided him in working with his post-traumatic stress.

The daily interaction with nature was often a spiritual event for people in the distant past. The cyclical nature of time returned each individual to the beginning of creation, as creation was demonstrated in the renewal of the seasons. Many ancient people regarded the universe as a living organism and sometimes even saw little differences between themselves and the earth. They viewed any event in their daily lives as a manifestation of magic, not uncommon in a world filled with daily wonder. They saw the universe as alive and connected by a shared direction.

Far from the cold, disconnection of the modern person, the ancients believed in the interconnection of all things. It was in this interconnection that the potential for magical events occurred. They believed that when people were not in connection with the flow of the natural world, they experienced strife and hardships. When this happened people were in a spiritual hell. If those same afflicted people changed their actions to harmonize more with the course of nature, then they would experience heaven on earth. To these ancient people heaven was in the earth, not a place people went to after death.

The modern elimination of purpose and meaning from our lives has led many to a view of the universe as dead, meaningless, and lacking any possibilities for magic or mystery. Instead of viewing the world as interconnected and alive, many in the modern world see the universe in terms of separation and lifelessness. There is no place for magic and all events are random and without meaning. I believe this view of our world directly affects how we interact with others. If we view this universe as nothing but dead matter, we often feel indifference and alienation from, not only our natural world, but also from other people. We become observers of nature instead of active participants. We fall for what the writer, Colin Wilson, referred to as the "fallacy of insignificance."

The Greek philosopher Plato believed the world was a living creature in which people are but one of its parts, connected with all the other parts. Nature holds patterns which cannot be seen from our limited perspective. All parts, both living and non-living, play a role in a vast system: neither are isolated entities. We can see that every living thing has a connection to every other living thing if our perspective becomes wide enough.

Living a magical life involves opening our minds to recognize we are a part of a vast system which needs us as we need it. If we design our lives to flow with the system then things will go so much more smoothly in life. However, if we ignore our part in the whole, things can become strained at best. Our actions, can affect this system so choosing actions which benefit the whole not only allows us to meet our needs but the needs of the system as well. This is often identified as "karma". Essentially, allowing life to flow with nature can decrease many of the blocks we experience to our health and happiness. By completing certain actions and altering certain patterns we can obtain the necessary inner resources to create massive transformations in how we view ourselves. These inner transformations can then lead to outer transformations in the areas of our relationships, finances, careers and spirituality. It is only by giving ourselves access to these inner resources can we really truly change as people. And this change can benefit our world.

When we view our world as created by a force outside

of nature we have essentially created a belief system that asserts a deep separation between us and the natural world. For many people a belief that there is a creator outside of its creation has led to short sighted and destructive actions which have fueled a belief system of disconnection between humans and nature. If we are not a part of the creation, we can then only continue to feel separation and existential angst as we attempt to navigate this strange world.

In his book, "God is Red", Vine Deloria, Jr. argues that Western perceptions of divinity being outside of nature have created a lack of spiritual connection to the land in our culture. He asserts that the concept of a God to whom the natural environment has no real significance, has caused the view of the natural world as having no relevance. This shift in thinking has made the very land we inhabit into something that is not worthy of regard. The spiritual relevance of nature is something most ancient cultures shared but has since been collectively lost. Our focus today is on using nature as if it were something outside of ourselves.

This kind of thinking has resulted in the mechanistic view of the world which has dominated over the last several hundred years. Many view the natural world as something to be governed and directed rather than something with which to be in harmony. Our desire to dominate our environment rather than to exist as a part of it has not only had adverse environmental repercussions but also has led to our feeling that something is missing in our lives. Our desire to control something that we cannot control has led to our collective feelings of anxiety, which impedes creativity and magical possibilities.

The truth is that nature becomes more and more mysterious, as quantum physicists delve into the world of the subatomic. Many scientists are beginning to believe that the universe is not random or meaningless but may be alive and purposeful. Research findings over the last one hundred years in the discipline of quantum mechanics have suggested that the universe is far from a mechanistic process but may be much more complex and multidimensional than was assumed.

Quantum mechanics has shown us that the universe may be stranger than we thought. This field has recognized that there is a relationship between the mind of an observer and activity at the quantum level. Researchers have found that subatomic particles sometimes behave specific ways based on the perception of the experimenter who is observing the particles. This has led many to the conclusion that the world we inhabit is not strictly outside ourselves. We are an active part of the world and our perceptions are interconnected with the world. There is not "outside" world and there is no "inside" world other than our perceptions.

We may feel that there is a world strictly outside of ourselves but any quantum physicist will inform you that what is really outside ourselves is a vast assortment of subatomic particles. These particles are interacting with our five senses which create a fluctuation of chemicals in our nervous systems. These fluctuations create flows of information which produce a large variety of images and sensations in our minds. The images and sensations are often not what it happening outside of ourselves but are, in reality, constructed by our minds from the sensations we are receiving.

All of this shows us that nature is us and we are nature. We cannot be separate from that of which we are a part. Any action we take is a part of interaction with nature. In order to find harmony in our lives we need to understand that it is by acknowledging our interconnection with nature that we can find our place in the world. Nature affects us and we affect nature. We are what we seek. It is a very simple concept, but when we truly accept this concept, a tremendous shift occurs which gives us a key to living in happiness and harmony with the world.

To begin viewing ourselves as part of nature, we must observe and reflect on things differently than we have been programmed to do. It can be difficult to unchain our minds from socially conditioned beliefs so we need to become very curious about this world and notice what we have not previously noticed. By performing these exercises you will become more open to the idea that there is an implicit order in the way nature works and that you are part of that order. If you allow yourself to open your mind to a different perspective, you may find that even aspects of the world you might have previously thought of as mundane can be seen as magical.

The results for these exercises should be recorded in a journal. I recommend buying a special journal that you will only use to record your ideas and experiences as you work through the exercises in this book. This will be a special journal which you can use on your magical journey through life.

Exercise #1: Seeing from the Center Out exercise

Find a quiet place where you will not be disturbed for ten to fifteen minutes. Sit down where you can be comfortable but remain alert. Take a minute or two to breathe deeply and begin to slow your breathing down.

Close your eyes, and in your mind envision the room in which you are sitting. Allow your mind to remember all the details of the room and where you are located in the room. Fully experience yourself being in the room. Fully experience all the incoming information from your senses as you sit quietly. Just enjoy being present in the moment.

Now, allow your awareness to move outside the room while also continuing to experience being inside the room. Let your mind spread outside the room to include your home.

After you have accomplished this, now let your mind envelope the area outside your home. Feel that these areas outside your home are as much a part of you as is your home and the room where you are sitting.

After you have fully experienced being a part of the area outside your home, then incorporate a part of your neighborhood. After you have done this, then include your city. Continue to expand your awareness to fully include the country you are in and then the continent in which you live.

Finally, include the Earth itself as part of yourself. Notice what it feels like to fully embody the Earth. Allow yourself to experience yourself as the totality of the Earth. You can then allow yourself to experience being a part of the universe.

After you have completed this exercise, sit quietly and process what your emotional experience was during the exercise. Write down your experience in your journal and read it daily.

Exercise #2: Read about Ecology

Go to your local library or bookstore and obtain a book on the subject of ecology. Take your time reading it. Make sure you fully understand each section of the book and see the connections between the natural world and the species which inhabit it. Notice how each species depends on each other to survive whether directly or indirectly. Investigate how a change in one specific plant can be a catalyst for a change in an entire species. See all the connections between all the species and how these connections operate with a wisdom outside of human direction.

Write down any thoughts in your journal you may have about the nature of your place in the ecological system. What connections are you now more aware of than before?

Exercise #3: Spend time with a tree

Go find a special tree that appeals to you and spend some time with it. Now before you think this is an exercise about being a new age "tree hugger," allow me to clarify what I am asking you to do. I want you to observe the tree and what happens to it and around it. How does this tree indirectly (or directly) affect you?

Trees have always had a place in different spiritual systems> Sometimes they were viewed as portals to the place of spirits or faeries. Buddha became enlightened while sitting under a Bodhi tree. The Bible had a tree of knowledge in the Garden of Eden which bore the fruit of knowledge. Many indigenous cultures have shamans who make spirit journeys to the center of the world which is known as a "cosmic tree." We hang ribbons from trees signifying special events. Trees have always had a special place in our imaginations.

Notice everything you can about the tree. Examine what small creatures live in or near the tree. Think about its root system underneath the earth. As you look at the tree think of this tree as a part of other trees with all of them forming a forest. See this individual tree as a part of a vast forest of which we are now a part. Allow the experience of being part of the forest sink in, and then envision a deep connection between the forest and all other parts of your life. Write down in your journal any emotions or thoughts which occurred as you performed this exercise.

Magical Life Principle #2 – Everything has Opposites

We often look at our world as being out of order or not functioning correctly. If we turn on the media these beliefs can be affirmed by the constant reporting of horrific events geared to capture attention. It is hard to live a magical life if we only see the events in our lives in a dichotomy of only good or bad. If our thinking is locked in dichotomies, then we leave little room for possibilities. If we do not understand that everything in the world has to have an opposite in order to exist, we create a perception of the world we inhabit as flawed or incorrect and that can cause us much despair and anxiety.

It is in having opposites that we can create a balance. Balance is something many people seek in their lives but cannot obtain due to a lack of understanding about opposites. We cannot have day without night. We cannot have good without having evil. We cannot have love without hate. We cannot have one side without the other. If we expect the people in our life to only be kind, we are usually disappointed and may find ourselves unable to have fulfilling relationships. If we seek new opportunities without expecting there to be challenges along the way, we can feel overwhelmed and unprepared. By acknowledging that everything we experience can also have the opposite qualities, we allow ourselves to have a more realistic perspective. This perspective gives us the ability to move with the ebb and flow of nature and avoid getting stuck with unrealistic expectations of how life should be. When we are freed from expecting a world that is one sided, we can embrace both sides in order to experience a magical life.

Many philosophers, such as Heraclitus and Anaximander, believed that it is by having opposites that our world can exist. The existence of an object or a situation depends on the existence of at least two conditions which are opposite of each other. These conditions, if balanced, will create a balance in the object or situation. If, however, one condition overpowers the other, then the strongest condition will dominate the weaker creating an unbalanced object or view of a situation.

The goal for many great thinkers throughout history was to hold the opposites in mind at the same time and view life from a different, higher perspective. They thought of opposites as part of a greater whole. By observing all things from this perspective, they found balance in all aspects of life. By seeing a great unity at the core of the opposites, they could navigate life's challenges by focusing pairs of opposites instead of viewing life as a one sided affair. It is by being open to both that we can go with the flow and see how things can work out in the long term. The Taoist principle of Yin/Yang also represents the concept of going with the flow of paired opposites in the world.

"Everything arises in this way, opposites from their opposites" – **Plato**

The creation of the universe itself is a wonderful example of the need for opposites. After the big bang our universe needed two opposite dynamics in order for life to appear. These opposing forces were expansion and contraction. After the big bang, matter moved away from where its' origin due to the force of expansion. If this force of expansion did not have an opposite force to stabilize it then no structures could have formed as everything would have been dispersed. Due to the opposing force of contraction, gravity, the matter which was moving away due to expansion was pulled back and stabilized. As a result of this contraction, structure was formed which eventually gave life to our universe.

Even in the realm of atomic particles we can see the necessity for opposites. Atoms are created due to opposite charges particles. The interaction of protons, which are charged positively, and electrons, which are charged negatively, create the conditions for the atom to exist. The charge of the protons and the electrons are the same size but must be opposites so the atom can exist.

In our own brains we need opposites so that our brain can function. For example, for a nerve cell to send a message down its axon, which is a long projection from the nerve cell, its inside must have a positive charge. If the nerve cell, however, needs the message to be inhibited, then the cell will become more negatively charged. If there were no ability to have both positive and negative charging in our nerve cells, then our brains would not function properly. It is only when the balance of these firings takes place that our brains can

37

function at optimum levels. We can also see the concept of paired opposites in the hemispheric aspects of our left and right brain. The left brain is commonly seen as a source of logic, reasoning, language and mathematical application, while our right brain is the source of creativity, artistic insight and emotions.

According to the depth psychologist Carl Jung, our minds have an innate propensity to place themselves through opposites which, when combined, can create a balanced whole. Jung believed in a principle called "enantiodromia" which presupposes that any force in the universe will eventually produce an opposite to itself. We need an opposite to exist in our lives in order to obtain harmony and balance. This is easy to see in the realm of relationships. Whether these relationships are personal or business, the same principle of opposites applies.

For example, if a company's Chief Executive Officer (CEO) is a person who has great ideas, she needs to be balanced with a Chief Financial Officer (CFO) who is grounded in the realities of economics and the marketplace. If the CEO wants to expand the company into areas it has not previously explored, it is up to the CFO to realistically determine the challenges to this shift in the company's operations and decide whether or not it would be in the company's best interest. If the CFO was not pragmatically grounded, then the company might suffer due to a lack of real world practical balance. The company would be chasing dreams which harmed the bottom line and result in economic failure. On the flip side, if the CEO shares the practical economic thinking of the CFO, then the company may not grow due to a lack of vision or too much focus on the bottom line. It is not uncommon to find companies that do not have leadership with a balance of opposites. These companies usually do not last long or at best survive, but do not thrive.

Recognizing and balancing of opposites is very necessary when entering into personal relationships as well. I have seen many couples in my therapy office with one complaining about their partners being totally different from him or her. These people believe that if their partners were just like them, then everything would function perfectly. I disagree with this idea. If there are not opposites in some areas of the relationship then the relationship will become out of balance and eventually stagnate. It is by embracing our differences and seeing these differences as part of a balanced whole that gives us contentment in our relationships. We should not be expecting our partners to exhibit the same thoughts, emotions and behaviors as we have.

If one partner is more relaxed, then she may need a partner who is more intense and energetic. She may be calm and centered but lack excitement and fun. Her partner, on the other hand, may be fun and energetic but lack grounding and focus. The blend of these personality traits will create a balance as the calm, relaxed partner will help ground the energetic, fun partner but the energetic, fun partner will help the calm, relaxed partner become more flexible and in touch with her emotions. If both partners were too relaxed then the relationship would become dull and boring. If both partners were energetic and only focused on fun, then they would lack long term vision. It is by having the opposites in the relationship that the relationship can become whole.

An introverted thinker may need a free spirited extrovert for help with becoming more alive. The reverse is true in that the free spirited extrovert will need an introverted thinker to consider all aspects of any important decisions made by the couple. We cannot grow as people if we are not challenged in a healthy way by the opposite of what we are. Our partners are here to respectfully challenge us to grow a little more in our comfort levels. Damning our partner due to his or her differences is a short sighted view of what it means to have a relationship. As long as the actions of our partners are not harming the relationship, then we may find their differences have lesson to teach us.

I once worked with a couple who felt they were on the verge of breaking up. It was obvious that neither had the ability to recognize the importance of a balance of opposites in their relationship. The wife, Cynthia, rattled off a long list of the things she was unhappy about in her husband, Tom. She stated that Tom was quiet, he didn't want to go out too often as he wanted to stay at home and relax, he didn't dance, he was more interested in learning technical material than artistic things, he was more conservative in his views, he was tighter with money, and he was a little more stern with the children than she was. Cynthia believed that because Tom was different there could be no common ground, and this would lead to the eventual dissolution of the marriage.

Tom did not understand the problems which Cynthia

40

laid out in the therapy session. He did not see why she needed to go out so much, why it was important to enjoy artistic things, why abandon his conservative views, why he should become less frugal with money, and why he should relax good boundaries with the children. He was unsure if Cynthia could love him for being himself or if he would have to become someone else in order to save their marriage. The thought of abandoning his sense of self was less than exciting to Tom.

After listening to both of them present their perspectives on their marriage, I asked Cynthia to tell me what benefits she enjoys from Tom's frugality with money. She instantly replied there was no benefit. I knew this could not possibly be true since everything has opposites. If there is a drawback there can also be a benefit. I pressed her to think of benefits. She eventually said that the when Tom handles the money there is always money available in savings. I then asked her the drawbacks if Tom handled money exactly the way she did. After some consideration she told me that if Tom handled their money exactly as she did, then there would be no savings and, possibly, more debt.

I then turned to Tom and asked him to tell me what benefits he could gain from staying at home less. Tom quickly replied that he didn't like going out much. I told him I understood, but he needed to think of the benefits if he decided to go out more. It took a good while, but Tom eventually said that he probably would have new experiences which might give him new ideas to implement in his work. I then asked Tom to tell me what were the drawbacks if

41

Cynthia wanted to stay at home as much or more than he did. He admitted that there would be more boredom and lack of interaction with the outside world if she modeled his reluctance to venture outside the home.

We continued to go through each of their issues one by one to find the drawbacks and benefits to each partner. When we were done with our session, Cynthia and Tom had a new appreciation for the balance which they had in their relationship. When they stop trying to make the other conform to their way of being, they could appreciate each other as they really are. They could also learn to benefit from the qualities which each one brought to the marriage. By being open to the big picture and being willing for opposites to exist, we can enjoy magical relationships.

I personally used the concept of exploring opposites while in the middle of the separation from my wife. I was depressed and overwhelmed with grief at her decision to leave our marriage. I felt a deep sense of despair that I had not experienced previously. One evening I decided to honestly and fully look at both sides of my situation in the hopes of finding some relief from my emotional pain.

I pulled out some paper and began writing everything I could think of that was negative about the ending of the relationship. I didn't censor myself while I was writing. There was a long list of all the things I was losing as a result of the impending divorce. I wrote down everything which was causing me pain. Tears flowed and fell on the paper as I wrote non-stop and allowed any thoughts and emotions to emerge.

When I finally stopped writing, I had filled up my papers with the long list of emotional losses.

I took a few breaths and then pulled out some more paper. I then started writing down all the things I would be gaining by the relationship ending. Initially I found it difficult to come up with much because I was so tied to the pain of emotional abandonment. After a little while, I found a few things floating around in the back of my mind to write. With those things now on paper, my mind then continued to freely supply other benefits resulting from the ending of the relationship. I was surprised how much I came up with because my thoughts had previously been consumed with my losses.

After writing down all the things I would gain by the ending of the marriage, I looked at the list of things I would be losing. I examined both lists thoroughly. I then sat quietly and just allowed myself to feel whatever I needed to feel. Different emotions came up and moved through me. I found myself holding fear, anger, curiosity and openness together which was really strange for me. A few minutes later, I found that my sadness was still there but so was something else, hope. There was a sense of hope that I did not previously have. There was hope for my future no matter who else was in that future. There was hope that I would be able to make it. I still hurt emotionally and would go through the usual stages of grief that accompany major life transitions, but there was now an inner resource to help me navigate through the difficult process. By being open to opposites, I was able to find some footing in this turbulent time. I was not happy but I

43

now had a new perspective to help me grow and move through the process.

Our lives will have highs and lows. Since we are a part of nature, we will have both creation and destruction in our life. We will experience good times and bad times. No situation is only good or only bad. By seeing a balance in whatever we are dealing with we can have a balanced perception as we navigate through our life.

Exercise – Balance the opposites

Write down a situation which you have previously thought as "bad". List all the things which caused you to view the situation as "bad". Take all the time you need to write everything you can think of and allow any emotions that come up to pass through without blocking them.

After you have completed writing the "bad" aspects of the situation, now write down all that has happened as a result of the situation that you could identify as good. This will be a challenge as we are programmed to think only one way about a situation, particularly an emotionally hurtful one. We frequently block our ability to see situations from a higher perspective. Commit to sitting and writing as long as it takes until you get a long list of positive outcomes from your situation.

When you have completed both lists, look at them at the same time. What do you notice differently about your situation now? The event has not changed, but what is your perspective now? Write down your thoughts and feelings in your journal and reflect on them over the next week.

Magical Life Principle #3 – Your Imagination Determines Your Magic

Our minds determine the quality of our lives. Everything we experience is connected at some level to the thoughts we are thinking. The more responsible we are for the quality of our thinking, the more responsible we are for our own lives. If we truly want to change the conditions of our lives, then it is essential that we change the way we think. In order to have an experience radically different we have to give ourselves permission to first imagine it.

In using our imagination, we are entering the realm of spirit. We are going into a place where all things are possible. It is by entering into our imagination that we create magical lives. We find solutions to problems in our imagination previously thought unsolvable.

Imagination is often disparaged by our society. Someone who frequently utilizes imagination may be seen as out of touch with reality but this is not always so. We are out of touch with reality only when we remain in the realm of imagination. When staying grounded in the day to day reality of the physical world, we can also allow ourselves to experience unlimited magic in our imagination. This, helps us to become open to possibilities. It is in our imagination that

45

ideas begin the journey to physical form.

"The world of reality has its limits; the world of imagination is boundless." – **Jean-Jacques Rousseau**

Most of Albert Einstein's theories came not from laboratory experiments in the physical world, but rather from flights into the realm of his imagination. Plato believed that the human mind is connected to a universal mind whose imagination gives rise to creations from the divine. Neo-Platonists believed our minds are part of a "cosmic mind" which create and direct all the physical properties that cause all things in the universe to exist. They believed this cosmic mind is outside the realm of space and time. This corresponds to the realm of our own imagination. We can do anything within our minds. We can find unlimited possibilities. It is the enjoyment many of us had as children, but have lost touch with as we become "responsible" adults. If the Neo-Platonists were correct, imagination is not merely just a flight of fancy but an extension of the cosmic mind which can create many remarkable effects.

"The quality of the imagination is to flow, and not to freeze." – **Ralph Waldo Emerson**

Experiencing our imagination can cause the same neurons to fire as if we were experiencing what we are imagining first hand. By imagining ourselves participating in a specific event, our brains will activate the same chemicals as if we are actually having the event. Having an active imagination increases our ability to have a magical life. If we cannot imagine new and exciting things to happen to us, then we wander through life feeling lost and disconnected from our potential.

Think of your imagination as an oracle that only works for you. The Oracle at Delphi, the Pythia (or priestess) was completely open to whatever information came to her. She did not censor the images and sensations she experienced, but rather honored them and shared them as she believed they were part of the divine. We too often hesitate to use our imagination and instead stay rooted in drudgery of "reality". By being open what appears in our imagination, we find ourselves with a more curious and playful attitude toward life.

When we are open to the realm of imagination, we give ourselves a gift. In our imagination we can accomplish or create anything. In our imagination we can create wonderful outcomes to difficult situations. Everything begins in our minds and in our imagination. In order to enhance who you are and what you can become, you must access and utilize your imagination. To become the director of your magical life, make a conscious effort to allow yourself to freely imagine all types of opportunities and possibilities without censoring yourself. Notice how good you can feel when you envision positive outcomes and surprising endings to different situations in your life. Your inner world will be reflected in your outer world (which we will discuss in more depth in the next chapter).

Exercise – Imagination Free Flow

Take some quiet time in a place where you will not be disturbed for ten to fifteen minutes.

Close your eyes and sit back comfortably. All you need to do is watch your mind. Give yourself permission to allow your mind to drift to wherever it goes. If you have a specific problem to solve, give your mind permission to freely flow into the realm of imagination looking for a solution. Take the role of observer as you follow the mind's travels. Do not become attached to what you witness, just allow it to happen. If things appear to become a little strange in your imagination, continue to observe without emotional attachment. You may be surprised what ideas and images come forth during this time. It is rare that we give our mind full permission to enter the world of imagination.

If people or objects appear, try to engage in a dialogue with them. Are there messages for you? As silly as this may sound, it can work wonders in opening up your mind to new possibilities. Be receptive to all things which want your attention during your imagination time. You do not have to follow any directives which are given to you in the imaginal realm, so just be open and enjoy the process.

After you have completed this short excursion into your inner world, write down in your journal anything that stood out to you. Do this exercise daily. The idea for of this book came from this very exercise. When I have recommended this simple exercise to clients, they often balk at it at first. After reluctantly doing it a few times, they usually find they enjoy their imagination time. They sometimes find answers to problems unsolvable until they decide to go within.

Magical Life Principle #4 – Our Focus Creates the Quality of Our Lives

What we focus our attention on is what usually grows in our lives. Think of this like the watering of a garden. The plant you are watering usually grows, and what is not being watered does not grow. Whatever our focus is on will often create more of it in our lives. The quality of our experiences is impacted by what it is we focus on. Becoming aware of where our attention is placed is a prerequisite for creating a magical life.

Our society wants us to focus on the important. A society fascinated with accumulating insignificant junk will direct its focus on how to obtain such things. A society which is focused celebrity drama will focus on outlets supplying that information.

Our attention dictates what we experience, so in order to have more of what we want we must focus more on what we desire. As one of my mentors used to say, "You can never have enough of what you don't want." If you focus on the worst, then you will get it. When we choose to focus on the unpleasant aspects of our lives we will experience more unpleasantness. If, however, we focus our attention on what makes us happier, then we will experience more happiness. It is a simple idea but often we are not aware of where our focus is directed. We notice how things are not working in our lives and paying little attention to what is working.

By choosing where our focus goes we create the conditions for magic to occur. Acknowledging that our experience of life is due to what we focus on, we can begin to assert enormous power to change the quality of our lives. In order to use the power of focus to create magical lives we need to answer one question, "What is really important to you?" Our priorities in life will determine how we focus our mind and set our expectations. Our priorities will dictate what opportunities we will see. If we are focused on what is really important to us, then we will find more opportunities to fulfill that desire. Everyone will naturally focus on what is truly a priority. Even if we say something is a priority, it is our actions which indicate what is important.

I see this all the time in my work as a psychology instructor at a local college. Students tell me their studies are a priority to them, but their actions tell me this is not true. These students are lying to me. They believe that their studies are a priority, but they are so out of touch with themselves and unaware of where the focus goes. They may spend hours a day watching television but then complain about a lack of time for studying or too much reading to do. The truth is that their studies are not their real priority; they just believe their studies are a priority. Their priority is leisure time and television, and they do not recognize this at all.

When someone else's focus is on something different from yours, they have a different set of priorities. When we expect others to have the same priorities as we do, we are usually very disappointed. Remember that no one will ever have exactly the same priorities as you. In order for the world to work, people must have a wide variety of priorities. If a medical doctor has the same priorities as a plumber, then the doctor will not focus on important aspects of her job. The same goes for the plumber. What people prioritize in their minds is what they will focus on. People who live magical lives consciously focus on the things which are most important to them. By consciously deciding what is a priority in our lives, we can then use the power of focus to create a life of abundance and happiness.

Magically living manifests when you are crystal clear about what your priority is and feel free to choose your own priorities. Few people know their true priorities and even fewer consciously decide to follow them. Often when people discover where they have been putting their energy in their lives; they are horrified since it is not what they truly want for themselves. Aligning our focus to what we truly want creates a change in how we interact with the world. We may decide that many of the things we used to believe were so important may no longer matter anymore. I have seen this when people are confronted with the death of a loved one or their own impending death. These people suddenly wake up to their most important priority. They may have been overly focused on material accumulation, but now they may shift their focus to family interactions.

There are times when we cannot motivate ourselves to perform certain tasks because these times are not a priority to us. When we are clear on what our priorities are, we can then have a better understanding of what type of tasks we need to do and what type of tasks we need to assign to others. If we are doing work that is not truly a priority for us or in a relationship that is not our priority, then it is very common to see a lack of initiative on our part.

An example of this is a former client of mine named Julia. Julia was a wonderful woman about fifty years old who was having trouble staying motivated in her work as a mid-level manager in a large company. She was beginning to be depressed about her life in general. She complained of the "inability to focus on the big picture" at work and of a feeling of not being in synch with her management. She was showing signs of burnout and despair. She told me that all she wanted was to just begin enjoying her life again. She was down on herself and did not understand what was wrong with her.

After listening to her for a little while, I asked her to tell me about a time when she felt really alive and fully in the moment. She told me she couldn't remember one. I pressed her to go back in her mind to a time where she was really alive and engaged in something that was a priority to her. She thought for a minute and then told me that she was a senior in high school and was competing in dance competitions. She loved dancing and used to teach dance at a school. Her physical state began to change before my eyes as she went into detail about dance competitions she performed in and how she instructed her students. She looked and acted so different from the woman who had come in my office twenty minutes earlier.

I asked her when was the last time she danced, to which she replied, "It seems like forever." I asked her why. She then told me about some negative things that had happened at the dance studio many years ago and how she had moved away from dancing and become more involved in the work she was now doing. As she talked about her present life, her body resumed the slumped depressed posture she had when she walked in the room earlier. I clearly saw the problem. She was a dancer not a mid-level manager. She was also a teacher. Her priorities were not being honored so her focus was on something uninspiring to her.

I thought for a moment and then asked Julia if she would be willing to do something to change how she felt. She replied she would be willing to do most anything within reason. I told her to go buy magazines related to the art of dance and cut out any pictures in the magazine that resonated with her. She was then to create several collage posters that she was to put in a room in her home where she spent the most time. She was to sit quietly in the room and just look at the poster collages of all the dancers for ten minutes in the morning and ten minutes at night. I then immediately dismissed her from the session with the assurance that she should come back to see me in three weeks to let me know how she was doing.

Three weeks later Julia returned and I could instantly tell something was different about her. She sat down and then proceeded to tell me how for the first two days she refused to do the collage because she thought the assignment was "silly." The third day something inside her told her that she needed to honor her commitment and do the task. She found several dance magazines and brought them home along with poster board. She found pictures which she liked and then cut them out and glued them to the board. She then put them in her bedroom and sat and looked at them the requested amount of time.

After the third day of sitting in her room looking at the pictures, Julia felt something shift inside her. A small voice from the back of her mind asked her why she didn't dance at home. She immediately got up out of her chair and put on some music. She danced around her whole house. With every moment of dancing she began to feel more connected to herself. By the time she had finished dancing she was exhausted. She was surprised to see that she had danced for over two hours! The time flew by, and she didn't realize it.

After that experience, she began dancing on her own every day. She also decided to call up a local organization which participated in dance competitions and volunteer her services. After finding out her background in dancing, they asked if she would eventually like to be considered for a judge position at competitions. She instantly said yes to this idea. Within a week she was interacting with dancers of all ages and experiencing the world of dance again. She was truly alive as she rediscovered her priority.

Julia told me she no longer felt depressed. She was much happier at work and now viewed her job as a way to pay for dancing excursions which made the time at work more enjoyable. She was a changed person when she became clear on what her true priorities were. She eventually moved to another state where she had more success working behind the scenes with dancing competitions.

When we are truly clear about our priorities, we can focus our minds so much more easily on getting what we truly want. If you are unclear about what your real priorities are, I would recommend doing the exercises below. The following exercise will help you to discover what you want to focus on.

Exercise - Priorities of Time

Write down what you do with your time when you are not fulfilling outside obligations. If you do not have to focus on anything specific, what do you find you catch yourself doing? Write down all the things you really get excited about in your life. Even if you think it is silly, write it down. Take as much time as you need as long as you are being sincere on what things make you excited.

Now look at all the things you wrote down and begin finding a specific time to engage in these activities more often.

Commit to doing more of the things that are your true priority for two weeks. After two weeks have gone by, notice how differently you feel about your life. Write in your journal any changes you have noticed since you began honoring your true priorities more often.

Magical Life Principle #5 – Our Words Create Magic

Most of us don't realize the power our words hold. Words build messages to understand each other. With words we can create amazing connections with others. We can also use our words to emotionally wound people deeper than if we physically struck them. In my therapy practice I have seen firsthand how the use of words can help people heal and transcend their present emotional troubles. Careful reflection on the words we use when talking to others, as well as ourselves, holds great rewards and can transform our lives. The archetypal magicians from old myths and stories cast spells with their words knowing the power that the spoken word carries.

Words don't exist in the physical sense. They are merely symbols to refer to what we perceive around us. An original component of human communication is our ability to utilize these symbols. One of the biggest differences between most animals and humans is that we are able to adjust our thinking into a form of communication that entails specific utterances that represent objects and concepts. Our words allow us to be more aware of our thoughts in a manner which animals cannot. Having a word for a situation, object or group can alter the level of attention we give to it and the way in which we categorize it.

"No matter how eloquently a dog may bark, he cannot tell you that his parents were poor but honest" –Bertrand Russell

The connecting component between language and thought is meaning, and the meanings we create are versatile and adjustable. We all have thoughts that cannot be expressed verbally. Babies have thoughts without having a language to express those thoughts. Even as adults most thoughts and meanings are almost unconscious to us. Without language we would not be fully aware of our thoughts. We would know what is happening but not the meaning it holds for us.

A powerful way to change our thinking is through the use of our words. When we verbally instruct our mind to focus on a specific desired outcome, we increase our ability to generate that outcome. Different cultures use words, such as mantras, chanting or specific prayers, in a variety of ways to change their emotional states. The use of rhythm with spoken words can create altered states and open us to new experiences.

Words can direct one's consciousness in various directions. We have all had the experience of hearing a story which enrages us, saddens us, or makes us laugh out loud. The words that emanated from the speaker's mouth changed the way we felt in that moment. When we describe our own experiences, we are compelled to re-visit the initial experience with our accompanying emotions intact. If our words can have such an effect on how we feel and thus act, why don't we decide to take charge of our language and align it with our thoughts to create positive internal experiences for ourselves? If you decide to take conscious control of your words, you may find that you have more flexibility in how you experience the world.

In order to create a shift in our verbal patterns, we have to be mindful of what we habitually say to ourselves and to others. The simple act of paying attention to what we say can have powerful effects on how we react to our environment. Our use of specific words and phrases can be habitual and reactive. By paying attention to the words you use, you begin to notice that you may be limiting yourself in your responses to incoming information.

Here is an example. Notice how paying attention to what one is saying and then changing one's words can have a positive effect. I once worked with a woman named Teri who sought help for her constant negativity. No matter what was going on in her life, she consistently focused on the negative aspects of any situation. Anytime someone shared something new with her she immediately said something negative, such as "That won't work," "That is stupid," or "This is annoying." This alienated her from people she genuinely cared for in both her professional and personal life. I found that anything I said in our sessions was also quickly shot down in a series of pessimistic comments. She was so stuck in her pattern of verbal negativity that it occurred without conscious thought.

One day I asked Teri if she would be willing to do something for a few weeks that could possibly change how she interacted with others. I told her it would not be easy, but it was something she could gradually become accustomed to doing. With some trepidation she asked me what she should do. I told her that for the next three weeks anytime someone asked her about something or shared anything new with her, no matter if it were bad or good, she was to say out loud, "That is interesting." So if someone asked her what she thought of a business proposal, personal situation or another person's actions, the first thing she was to say was "That is interesting." After that she was free to say what she felt she needed to say. She just had to pause and say those three words first. I even gave her a job of looking at any object she saw on her way to work every day and say to herself, "That is interesting."

After a couple of weeks of performing this new task, Teri noted some small changes in how she related to others. Even though she still had a large dose of negativity, she found that she wasn't always quite so quick to be negative. She found that her thoughts didn't immediately go to a negative comment. She had a little flexibility in her words which led to more flexibility in other areas of her life. Teri continued to be mindful of her words which, in time made her more approachable to others. This change helped her in making friends and maintaining good interactions with co-workers.

Try this exercise for a week and see what happens for you:

As you go through your day notice something that you usually pass over. As soon as you notice it, say to yourself,

"That is interesting." You may be driving to work and pass a stand of trees that you rarely pay attention to, but this time notice the tress and immediately say to yourself, "That's interesting." Do the same to things you see that are not pleasant, like an ugly truck stop or a bland strip mall. Over time notice how you have become more aware of the world around you and how your first reactions may shift.

When we align our words with our thoughts we create momentum toward changing our lives. If we have thoughts which work for us we can experience tremendous changes in our emotions. When we accompany these changes in thought with shifts in our language supporting more positive, resourceful thinking, our nervous system adjusts our outlook on the world even more. Like the magicians who cast spells using words, you are creating a minute by minute spell which affects your reality. You are creating either a compelling reality or a disdainful reality by your vocabulary.

Begin noticing your words today. Notice words which align with your highest ideals for yourself and continue using them. If you find that certain words do not create emotional connection to the person you would like to be, omit them from your language. For example, a friend of mine noticed he often used the word "bored." He did indeed feel bored, but he wasn't sure that his constant use of the word didn't enhance the feeling of being bored. He began to substitute the word "curious" for the word "bored." When asked how he felt, he no longer replied that he was bored. He merely responded that he was feeling curious. Over time he noticed his curiosity increased, and his boredom decreased. He had more out of the box ideas about his business and hobbies, and he was far from feeling bored.

Exercise – Word shifts

Begin noticing words that you use that disempower you, and begin replacing them with alternate terms which give you more possibility in how you could feel.

For example:

The word "PAIN" can be replaced with "DISCOMFORT." They both have similar meanings, but one may be easier to bear. The word "SAD" can be replaced with "PERPLEXED". The word "AFRAID" can be replaced with "CAUTIOUS." The word "ANGRY" can be substituted with "FRUSTRATED."

See how many words for which you can find alternate terms for in your conversations. Pay attention to any shifts in how you feel after a few weeks of adopting a new vocabulary.

Magical Life Principle #5 – Our Actions Are What Create the Conditions for Magic to Occur

"In the absence of willpower the most complete collection of virtues and talents is wholly worthless." -Aleister Crowley

Now that we have balanced our perceptions, focused our priorities, opened up our imagination, and added flexibility to our words, the next thing task to begin creating a magical life is to add action. When we have aligned our thoughts, words and actions with laser like focus, our goals become more easily obtained. Yet, action is the very area where most people have problems. They may have changed their thoughts and words, but they seem helplessly stuck in either inaction or taking action in habitually limiting ways.

Perhaps you know someone who spent money on self-help books and self-help seminars, but the person never takes action in changing. Unfortunately, many people believe it is a lack of information which keeps them from reaching their goals so they continue to buy books and go to seminars but they fail to act.

Why do so many of us fail to take action toward creating the life we desire? I believe that the main reason is that we have such ingrained patterns of behavior that to begin doing something different feels like an insurmountable task. If for years and years we have done something a specific way, then we think it is too difficult to change. We believe we are old dogs attempting to perform new tricks. Our lack of new action only solidifies undesired patterns of behavior. No matter how many wonderful thoughts and words we may think and speak, if we do not take an action in alignment with those thoughts and words, we will be unable to reach our desired result.

Think of how we behave as a recipe. We behave in set

pattern much like a recipe to prepare a dish. If we mix in too much of one spice or too little of another spice, the dish we prepare will not taste good. Our actions are like this. We must follow a "recipe" for how to do our behavior. We have to do certain things a certain way for the behavior will occur. This is good news because this means we can change the pattern with little adjustments, much like the spices in the dish. We can change the result of what we are doing. We open ourselves up to magical possibilities when we make adjustments to our habitual way of living.

I once had a therapy session with a woman named Sabrina. Sabrina exhibited obsessive compulsive behavior that caused her much distress. Anytime she heard news related to illness or to the medical field, she immediately had overwhelming panic about the possibility of her getting sick or dying. For some reason, unknown even to Sabrina, the only way she could calm herself down and be able to focus on something else was to knock seven times on the nearest wall. If she did not do this, she would begin to feel a severe panic that erupted in shortness of breath and accelerated heart rate, basically a panic attack. The panic was overtaking her life. Even seeing a television commercial about medication caused her to get out of her chair and tap seven times on the wall. She was frustrated, embarrassed, fearful and tired of feeling she was out of control.

After hearing her problem I asked Sabrina how specifically she performs this pattern. I wanted to know her "recipe" for creating this behavior. After some discussion, she laid it out as follows:

63

1. See or hear something about illness or medicine either in person, in print or in the media

2. Have the thought, "That could happen to you! Maybe you are already sick and could die and don't even know it!"

3. Begin to worry about suffering from illness and dying which brings on a panic attack

4. Knock on the wall seven times to stop feeling so afraid.

Once I heard her simple "recipe", I knew that we only needed to change one small part as a beginning step toward helping Sabrina change. Instead of telling her that she must not knock on the wall anymore, I told her it was fine to knock on the wall, but she had to do one jumping jack between each knock for a total of seven jumping jacks. I then asked for her commitment to do what I asked of her for the next week. She agreed although she had little hope that this weird intervention would help her.

A week later Sabrina came back to her therapy session and told me that she had stopped knocking on the wall so often. She grew tired of having to do so many jumping jacks, and it was very inconvenient to do those when she was out in public. She had found the inner resources to resist the urge to knock on the wall. She still had a few thoughts about becoming ill, but these came much less frequently. She told me that her husband had begun counting her jumping jacks to ensure she did the required number. She was learning that the pattern that had ruled her life could actually be adjusted. Even though it was not a cure all for her anxiety, it was an important first step to overcoming the negative patterns which she had felt chained by in the past. I am happy to write that as of today she no longer has those obsessive compulsive symptoms. I may have helped to change her recipe, but she did the rest.

Many of us have patterns of behavior that are not in alignment with our thoughts and words. We may think "I am going to lose weight" and tell others "I am going to lose weight" but we find ourselves eating fattening food. In order to change our actions and to bring them more in line with our thoughts and words, we must adjust the way we act out our patterns. Even by creating small incremental adjustments to a pattern, big results can still follow. Play with your pattern and see what kind of results you can achieve.

Here are some examples of how one small adjustment in a pattern can achieve big results:

-I worked with a mother and teenage daughter who constantly argued for several hours every day. Both of them wanted the arguing to end but yet each felt compelled to continue yelling at each other for long periods of time every day. I directed them to feel free to continue arguing, but they must hold their arms straight up toward the ceiling anytime they were arguing. If one them got tired and began to drop her arms they both had to stop arguing. After three weeks of taking short breaks during their arguments due to the fatigue from holding their arms up, they found that they could more frequently stop arguing. They now had evidence that the pattern of non-stop yelling could end.

-A man came to see me for help with his weight. He was obese and claimed to be addicted to junk food. He told me he only ate the junk food at home at night while he sat in front of the television. I asked him to change the time when he ate the junk food to between the hours of 6am an 8am. He could only eat the junk during those times. After a couple of weeks he reported to me that he had decreased his intake of junk food by nearly half.

-The parents of a child who had uncontrollable tantrums sought help for the nightly anguish of dealing with an angry out of control eight year old. The child would throw a severe tantrum for nearly twenty minutes. They had tried everything to get the child to stop but nothing worked. The parents were directed to allow the child to have the tantrum but to insist that the tantrum must last ten extra minutes over the usual twenty minutes. The parents were to time the child to ensure the full thirty minutes was reached every night. This proved problematic to the child. Throwing a tantrum was hard work and the pressure of having to keep going with the tantrum was tiring. Eventually the pattern of tantrums began to disappear due to the change in how the parents responded.

As you can see, it does not take much to change our actions if we are curious enough about the recipe we use to create those patterns. Once we have broken a pattern, it is much like an old record album that has been scratched. The grooves of the record can no longer function the same way after the scratch. When this happens, it frees us for new actions which support us and move us in the direction of our goals. A magical life cannot happen if we don't put forth a magical effort to make things different

"I never worry about action, but only inaction."
-Winston Churchill

Magical Principle #6 – Synthesis of Mind, Word and Action Creates Real Magic

We have explored the principle of our imagination, our words, and our actions, we now must synthesize these three magical properties. One of the most simple and powerful ways to forge change in one's life is by using a principle called "The Three Mysteries." The three mysteries, or Sanmitsu as it is called in esoteric Japanese Buddhism, is the alignment of the powers of the intentions we set, the words we use to express those intentions, and the actions we take to bring the intentions to fruition. This concept is not limited to esoteric Buddhism but is also found in many different philosophical and religious writings.

Essentially, we only have three ways to create outcomes: through our thoughts, our words, and our deeds. All three of these work wonderfully at creating results. These results could be either really good for us or really bad for us. Our lives can become magical, or they can stay mundane based on how we choose to align our thinking, speaking, and acting.

Buddhism claims there are three dimensions; Dharmakaya (mind), Sambhogakaya (speech) and Nirmanakaya (body). These three are interconnected not independent of each other. In esoteric Buddhism, the three mysteries imply the purity of our conduct, words and thoughts. These are also known as the three vajras or the three gates. The greatest secret to these mysteries is that when one has fully coordinated all three components for a specific purpose, sometimes magical results can happen. If one aligns one's thinking, language and behavior to bring about change which matches the highest priorities in life, it is a force so great that it has little chance of failing.

The three mysteries are:

I-mitsu: focused intention – Becoming aware of the contents of the mind and transforming them.

Ku-mitsu: spoken vows – scared sounds/mantras

Shin-mitsu: action

The necessity for alignment between thought, word and action in order to create change in one's life explains why so many people do not create a life of contentment for themselves. Most people are completely unaware that their thinking, language and behavior can work in opposition to each other. They may try to think the right thoughts but are sabotaged by the actions they take which conflict with their thinking. They may try to improve their lives, but the words they use to direct their actions disrupt the flow of effective activity. At best, they achieve minimal results with these disorganized attempts at change. Because people feel their energy is scattered due to this lack of congruency. Most eventually give up and create justifications for their failure to generate their desired results. As a consequence many become mentally victimized by their lives and feel they have no control over what happens to them.

Kukai, the founder of Shingon Buddhism, believed if we comprehend the integral relationship between thought, word and action, then the same interrelated connection which exists between all things will become apparent. The great Persian sage, Zoroaster, believed it is by having good thoughts, speaking good words and doing good deeds that we increase the presence of the divine force, which he referred to as "asha", in ourselves. All three mysteries have to work together if we are to generate a life we love. Empowering thoughts are great, but without action, they are impotent. Wonderful words can inspire but, without the inner thoughts that correspond with the outer words, we see no change. Actions can forge new ways of being in the world, but without the accompanying thoughts that support such actions; eventually the initiator becomes uninspired and ceases such activity.

In order to understand how these three mysteries work together, we must understand how each one operates individually. By examining the power of each area, we can discover how we have been limiting ourselves. The more we recognize the immense power we inherently possess, the more we can learn to direct it toward goals that move us in the direction of living an inspired and magical life.

So how do we put together all three components of the "Three Mysteries" in working toward a magical life? It is a simple process that can create amazing outcomes. Even though it is simple, it does require diligent focus and determination to activate a synthesis between our thoughts, words and deeds. Let's go through the process:

Step 1 – The first treasure is our thoughts. Everything begins in the mind. If we can fully experience positive resourceful thoughts, then we can begin building a mind that automatically works toward our goal.

Decide what you want to have, do or be. Think about your goal in as specific way as possible. Notice what emotions come forward as you think about it. Notice what images emerge as you think about your goal. Examine your thoughts to ascertain if the goal is truly something that you want. If you notice part of you has objections, examine those objections to ensure whether or not they are legitimate objections or just fear rising at the prospect of change. If you do indeed believe the goal you have chosen is in alignment with your highest values, begin envisioning the completion of the goal in vivid detail. Notice any sounds or feelings in your vision that would accompany the completion of your goal. Intensify all positive emotions associated with the goal. Hold onto those feelings for as long as possible.

Step 2 – The second treasure is our words. By aligning our language with our thoughts we move closer to creating our lives as we wish them to be.

Once you have envisioned the completion of your goal, you now move to the realm of words. Begin stating out loud to yourself what the outcome of the goal will be like. Write it down on a piece of paper and hang it in an area you see every day. Every time you see the paper with the goal written on it, say it out loud to yourself several times. You may also share this goal with others who support you and can add encouragement. Every day read and repeat your goal to ensure that you stay focused and aligned with your thoughts. Imagine that you are creating your own magic spell.

Step 3 – The second treasure is our actions. By taking consistent action in the same direction as our thoughts and words, we can bring about the results of our choosing.

Take your goal and break it down to several specific steps that are needed to obtain it. Break the steps into smaller portions so you are doing some small action every day toward the completion of the goal. Create a daily ritual in which you complete a specific step toward obtaining the goal. If you have a pattern of action which limits your ability to reach your goal, then begin making small adjustments to those patterns.

This process is a simple process but one which requires focus and dedication. Here is an example of how one could use the process to manifest a goal in his or her life:

Clara is working at a job she does not enjoy. It pays the bills

71

but gives her no satisfaction in her life. She has always wanted to become a nurse but never has acted on her dream. One day she feels that she is ready to move forward and start the process of working in the nursing field.

Step 1 – Clara thinks about being a nurse in extreme detail. She envisions herself working in the hospital attending to patients in vivid detail. She sees herself in her nursing scrubs filling out charts and interacting with the families of the patients. She allows herself to feel how she would feel if she were performing those tasks. She increases the intensity of the good feelings and imagines these scenarios for five minutes in the morning and five minutes in the evening every day.

Step 2 – Clara writes down the following on a piece of paper: "I am a nurse working in a hospital where I make a great income while helping people feel better." She then hangs this paper on her bathroom mirror where she sees it every morning. Out loud she recites this sentence to herself. She then tells friends whom she trusts about her goal and asks for their encouragement. Every day she states out loud the affirmation she has written to herself to reinforce it in her mind.

Step 3 – Clara takes her goal of becoming a nurse and breaks it down to a series of steps that she can perform easily. She lists such steps as calling her local college to get information about the nursing problem, applying to the school, checking into financial aid, setting up time to study, placing some of the money from her present job into a savings account for her to use when she is working at her internship, etc. Each of these steps are assigned dates of completion to make sure she is consistently taking action on her goal.

As you can see, this is an active process which can yield great results if consistently utilized. Many people only get as far as Step One before they become complacent or distracted and never complete the other steps. In order for you to create magical outcomes in your life, it is essential that you use your thoughts, words and actions together to yield your desired outcomes. When these are aligned, it is like a superhuman force rising up within us. We can construct our lives in a manner we would not have previously believed possible.

"The thought manifests as the word. The word manifests as the deed. The deed develops into habit. And the habit hardens into character. So watch the thought and its ways with care. And let it spring from love, born out of concern for all beings." ~The Buddha

Magical Principle #7 – Life is an Alchemical process

Alchemy has its early roots in the ancient traditions of Northern Africa. It spread throughout the world due to the influence of the Islamic Empire. The laboratory practices of alchemy found their way into parts of European culture which were fascinated with the search for understanding of the laws of nature and humanity's place in the cosmos. The outward processes of alchemy were the forerunner to modern chemistry. Many sought to use the techniques of alchemy for the transmutation of base metal into gold. No one was successful in this endeavor. On further investigation, it appears that many alchemists were not just interested in turning metal into gold but also to produce the "gold" within themselves. This specific form of gold was in reality merely a symbol for the practitioner's advancement in the spiritual realm.

Many alchemists were interested in the spiritual aspects of what they called "The Great Work." This was a spiritual and philosophical process in which these aspirants worked to transform themselves into a divine being by learning the hidden secrets of nature. This work culminated in the creation of something alchemists called "the philosopher's stone." The creation of the philosopher's stone is a metaphorical process of obtaining greater awareness and peace in one's life. This process was cloaked in mysterious and archaic symbols only known to those initiated into the secrets of alchemy. During the time alchemy gained a foothold in Europe, the prevalent power in society was the Christian church which did not take too kindly to those who practiced alternative spiritual practices. As a result, the alchemists used symbols to represent their unique terminology, avoiding any potential unpleasantness from the ruling establishment.

This spiritual process of alchemy begins with a person experiencing an ordinary existence. His life is going the same as it usually goes, without many surprises and much change.

The individual then begins to have experiences which transform his mental, emotional, and physical essence. He becomes more aware of different aspects of his being. He begins to shed old concepts about himself, much like a snake shedding its skin and becomes open to new energies and ideas about the world around him and begins to allow new information about who he really is to take root. This leads to new insights about his place in nature and the purpose of his life. The essence of "The Great Work" is the expansion of perception and awareness about oneself.

This process is a fundamental part of nature and a fundamental part of our lives. If we open up to this process, we can reap rewards. However, if we fight it, then we remain at the same level of personal growth, we make matters worse by attempting to hold on to a life that no longer exists causing us deep emotional pain. By becoming aware of the alchemical process of life, we can adapt to and flow with these changes and even thrive through what we initially believe is chaos. We feel that our lives have become chaotic when we are shown aspects of ourselves which we did not know existed or did not wish to acknowledge. It is by embracing change and allowing this process to occur that we can truly move upward.

The first stage of the alchemical process is called "nigredo" or blackening. This stage is when the alchemist begins to destroy the original metal, called the "prima materia", so that impurities in the substance can be removed. Metaphorically, the impurities are our old selves or identities which no longer serve us. This stage is when we find that our old lives do not satisfy us anymore, and we desire or are forced to begin a process of change. This change is never easy. It is often very painful and stress producing. St. John of the Cross referred to this period as the "dark night of the soul." Even though our old lives no longer served us, we yearn for the familiar and the illusion of permanence. When we do not have those things we mistakenly believed were permanent, we often feel a shift into depression and/or fear. These feelings were represented by alchemists in symbols such as a solar eclipse, darkness, or a black raven. This is the death of the old self which is often emotionally painful and filled with perilous challenges.

I experienced this stage while I was dealing with the ending of my marriage. The life I had planned for myself suddenly disappeared. I had envisioned a long life with the woman I loved. Within a short period of time, my entire life had changed. I went from the role of husband and stepfather to being totally alone. My plans for the future disappeared, and I felt directionless. I initially fought this stage of my life with much fervor. I tried to reunite with my wife which was ultimately not successful. I would write down everything I had done in the marriage and find some way I could do things better. I would write out the pattern of conversations with my wife to discover how I could have been more accepting and peaceful when she was angry with me. I tried to give her time to change her thinking. All the things I tried ultimately failed. I was engulfed in the deepest amounts of despair I had ever experienced in my life. Life put me through the "blackening" stage pretty intensely. It was only when I decided to let go of my previous plans for my future that I was able to move forward to the next stage and to begin rebuilding my life.

Kyle, a client I worked with, struggled with this same stage. He had been employed by a local company for about eleven years. He had come to see his identity as an employee of this company. He was happy to have that identity since he enjoyed his work and the people with whom he worked. One day Kyle received word from the upper management that, due to the downturn in the economy, he and several of his co-workers would have to be let go from their jobs. This was devastating news for Kyle as he, not only had to deal with financial issues due to this change in his life, but he also had to find a new identity for himself.

Kyle struggled much more with the identity portion of this stage than with the financial. He was able to find work at another company but felt he was very unhappy. He didn't like the management or his co-workers as much as he did at his old company. He struggled with feeling depressed and directionless. In our work together we finally got to the root of the issue. Kyle needed to have a new identity, one not based solely on where he worked. This took time for Kyle to find out who he was and who he was becoming. He had to let go of the old image of himself as a lifetime employee of his old company. He had to embrace a new identity which would enrich his life. He began to connect more with his family and friends and found that his old identity did not include the important people in his life. He decided to let go of the "old Kyle" who was too focused on work and become open to the "new Kyle" who made his family and friends a priority. As a result, Kyle began to enjoy his life more and was surprised at how much better he enjoyed his new job when he let his old expectations go.

Situations like a divorce, loss of a job, or death of a loved one are parts of a process which strips away the old and gives us the new. The changing of our mental, emotional and physical conditions is a part of the ebb and flow of nature. As nature destroys, it will also create. The crops die off at the end of autumn only to be reborn in the spring. We go through hardships only to be reborn with a new life. This process can work for us only if we let go of the old. If we fight against it we will block our ability to learn and grow. By resisting the natural changes in life, we fight against the inevitable, which only makes our lives more difficult and painful. It is by allowing what "is" and giving away our old conceptions of how life "should" be that we arrive at a magical life.

Alchemical Nigredo Exercise: Give it away

To go with the flow of life we must be aware of different areas of our lives in which we are holding onto old things or people who no longer serve us. In order to prepare for moving into and through this stage, we must become comfortable with letting things go. To effectively open up to this alchemical stage, begin by letting go of small things in preparation for the large things we must let go of in the future.

Go through your closet, drawers, garage or storage

center and give away anything which you have not used in a year. If you have not used it in a year then you are more than likely not going to need it. Someone else may need it more than you, so let them have it. If something is there for only sentimental sake, then sit with it and see if you really benefit by holding on to the item. Sometimes our sentimental nature keeps us psychologically chained to the past and unable to move forward. By giving away old things which no longer serve us we open ourselves to new things which can bring us much more enjoyment and comfort, and constant accumulation of material things rarely gives us any long term happiness. The consistent quest for more usually leads to more debt and anxiety, two things most of us want to avoid.

I had a client named Diane who was going through a big shift in her life. Through our therapeutic work she became aware of how her desire to hold onto the past kept her from embracing her future. She decided to go into her closet and give away everything that she had not worn in a year. All was going well until she got to the back of her closet and found her wedding dress from her first marriage. The dress was still beautiful for much care had gone into making it. It was so nice that a similar dress would cost nearly a thousand dollars. She had held onto it for sentimental reasons. She attempted to put it in the pile to give away to a local charity but she found she couldn't do it.

When we discussed the wedding dress in our next session, she told me that she felt emotionally trapped by the dress but she didn't feel she could give it up. She felt she could not easily give up something that had meant so much to her. I encouraged her to take time and listen to her own emotions over the next two weeks which would tell her what she needed to do. I wanted her to make the right decision for her and not give away something because she felt she was supposed to complete a task.

When we spoke three weeks later, she told me that one night she woke up and had the thought that in order for her to let go of that part of her past, she needed to honor it before releasing it. The next morning she took the dress to the best dry cleaner in town and told them to do everything they could to get it as clean as possible. When she returned to the cleaner slater in the week, the dress looked even more beautiful to her. She took the dress home and hung it up in her bedroom.

Diane spent the day looking at the dress and checking in with what she was feeling. She came to the realization that the dress represented the change from being a young girl to becoming a woman. This had been a major milestone for her. Now as she approached middle age, she was entering into another stage. She saw that she was now becoming a woman of wisdom, since with age comes much wisdom. When she connected with the role of being a wise woman she was able to let the dress go.

She found a young woman at her church who was getting married in a year. This woman was a similar size to Diane when Diane originally had worn the dress. Diane gave the young woman with the dress with no expectations that the woman would want it or wear it. Seeing the dress, the young woman began to cry as she told Diane that she had always wanted to have a wedding dress like Diane's but she could not afford it. As soon as Diane heard this she knew she had made the right choice and was now able to move forward in her life. Over the next few weeks she found new opportunities for growth which she may not have been open to previously. When we allow ourselves to become unattached to impermanent things, we find that not only can we be happier with less but we can also be open to new possibilities.

The second stage of the alchemical process is known as "albedo" or whitening. In this stage the prima materia has obtained a level of fixedness. The material is now stable and cannot be destroyed. The fires which blackened the material previously can no longer affect the material. Metaphorically, in this stage of this process, we may find that our lives have been focused on things which do not really fulfill us. They may be unsatisfying relationships, career achievements or material possessions. The life which we have been living has lacked a deep connection with nature and with our own soul and spirit. We will want a new way of relating to ourselves, to others and to our world. We have let go of old hurts and expectations about our lives and have started to become open to new future opportunities. The more we open up to new possibilities, the more we find our true selves. Alchemists represented this stage with such symbols as the color white, a child, or the Moon.

When Kyle let go of his old identity and Diane let go of her wedding dress, they began to send a metaphorical message to nature that both were ready for the next phase of the adventure. The both wanted to move forward and begin a new life. They needed to drop their ideas about who they were and who they "should" have been and become open to what they could become.

Alchemical Albedo Exercise:

1. Write down all the aspects of your life that have been bothering you. Write down the things and situations that have kept you from living a magical life. Go into detail as much as possible. Write down the history of every block that impedes your living a magical life. Write down the name of any person who has wronged you in the past and whose influence has kept you from living a magical life. Take as much time as possible and don't censor yourself. Allow any old emotions to rise up during this exercise. Keep writing until you have written down every person and/or situation that has kept you tied to the past.

2. Go to the store and buy yourself a large white candle. Bring the candle home and sit with it for a few minutes reflecting on the color white and its place in the alchemical process of life.

3. Safely light the candle and use its flames to burn the papers on which you wrote down all the blocks you had in the past that kept you from living a magical life.

4. As you watch the papers burn, reflect on the destruction of the paper as the destruction in the Nigredo stage.

5. Take the ashes and find a special place that only you know about and bury them. As you bury the ashes reflect on their becoming part of the earth and taking part in the endless cycle of destruction and creation.

The final stage of the alchemical process is "rebudo" or reddening. This is when the alchemist ensures that the white matter from the previous stage becomes even more stable to the point of being completely fixed. Metaphorically, this stage opens us up to higher levels of awareness about ourselves and our world. We discover our true selves and our purpose. We discover the magical parts of ourselves which are new to us or we had felt had long been lost. In this stage, we are becoming architects of our own lives rather than mere observers. Our awareness has increased and freed us from old, limiting programming. The symbols used by alchemists to represent this stage were the color red or a red stone.

Alchemical Rebudo Exercise

Spend twenty minutes sitting comfortably in a place where you will not be disturbed. Allow your mind to drift back over your life. Notice events which were important and observe them as part of an alchemical process. Observe where these events were in the nigredo stage, the albedo stage and the rebudo stage. Pay attention to how you felt during those times. Knowing what you now know about life as alchemical process, what could be different about your feelings during those times? With your new perspective, how might you respond to a similar situation? Write down your insights in your journal and reflect on your writing for ten minutes a day for the next week.

***

By practicing and cultivating these seven magical principles you will find that life becomes more interesting and enjoyable. You will gain a feeling of connection to the natural world and feel more in control of your life. In applying these basic principles you may find that life will take some surprising turns in undreamed of ways. You are just getting started on your journey.

CHAPTER 2: CULTIVATING A MAGICAL MIND

It is not uncommon in self-help literature to find reference to the power of thoughts. It has almost become a clichéd phrase in the genre that "your thoughts create your reality." However, there is some element of truth to this notion. In the realm of evidence based psychotherapy, research has shown time and again that changing people's thoughts can create changes in how they processes information which in turn has an effect on their emotions and behaviors. This shift in thinking can lead to how they interact with the world around them. How we think about our lives determines the quality of our lives. The ancients knew very well that our thinking impacts our lives since most every culture has some reference to the role of thought in how we interpret our world.

"Thought is subversive and revolutionary, destructive and terrible, thought is merciless to privilege, established institutions, and comfortable habit. Thought looks into the pit of hell and is not afraid. Thought is great and swift and free, the light of the world, and the chief glory of man." – **Bertrand Russell**

What is thought?

I define thinking as any mental activity involving a

person's subjective experience. Since thought determine our actions and reactions, one of the goals of psychology, philosophy, and biology, has been to discover where thought comes from and how it affects human development. It is thought that makes it possible for humans to be aware of and to understand the world around them. Thought interprets human existence and gives it significance.

What thoughts specifically are is a bit of a mystery since most experts can't come to a consensus on a workable definition. At the time of this writing, neuroscientists can agree that a thought is caused by brain activity, but it is still unclear what this activity does to create thought. Scientists are still attempting to learn if there are specific types of nerve cells that have an impact on thinking or if certain regions of our brain need to be mobilized to start the function of thinking. It is remarkable that with all our wonderful technology, we still cannot yet answer the very question philosophers have been debating for several thousands of years.

"We are what we think. All that we are arises with our thoughts. With our thoughts we make the world." - **The Buddha**

Our brains are remarkably complex structures. They are only about three pounds of soft tissue, but the level of their functioning is incredible. The activity that creates our conscious experiences occurs within the gray matter area, a covering of nerve tissue that surrounds the structures at the center of the brain. Gray matter is composed of neurons which are nerve cells that transmit information by way of electrical chemical signals called neurotransmitters. When a neuron fires it dispatches neurotransmitters across an open space between it and another neuron. This open space is called a synapse. After these chemical messengers cross the synapse, they may or may not be accepted by dendrites, which are special receptors on the next neuron. If accepted, the neurotransmitters fit in the receptor site like a key into a lock. Once accepted into the receptor site, this information is then spread to other neurons throughout the brain. It is these chemicals which affect our memories, learning and emotion.

Our brain's action is incredibly rapid and as a result is beyond the realm of our conscious awareness. Our conscious thoughts are only a small part of these rapid electrical actions. Modern neuroscience concludes that most of what we perceive is unconscious. Only a small part of what we experience is fully available to our conscious minds. Therefore, many of our decisions and thoughts are unconscious; we simply operate on autopilot without question.

I believe that the quality of our thoughts will determine the quality of our lives. From my work with many clients, I can testify to the difference a shift in thinking can do in changing a person's life. At the same time I have also observed that one can work on one's thoughts and see few changes. The reason this happens is because the majority of the thoughts are unknown to us and generally are not conscious. It is in this unseen realm of the mind where we find the keys to inner transformation.

"Man's status in the cosmos is determined by the quality of his thinking" – **Manly Hall**

The role of the conscious and unconscious minds

The conscious mind is the part of us of which we can be totally aware. For example, you are aware that you are reading at this moment. When you are speaking directly to another person, you are aware that you are talking. When you are outside your home, you are aware that you are no longer inside your home. You are aware of where you work. You are aware of what kind of automobile you drive. You are aware there are other people in your neighborhood. All of these situations you are completely aware, and this awareness is due to your conscious mind.

Your unconscious mind, however, is unknown to you. It is this part of your mind which controls involuntary processes such as the beating your heart and maintaining your breathing (imagine having to consciously remember to breath!). It knows just when to move your body into Rapid Eye Movement when you sleep. The unconscious mind also acts as an expectancy machine which is constantly scanning your environment to obtain information in order to decide what actions to take.

The unconscious mind might best be defined as that part of our minds which brings about an assortment of mental activity of which we are unaware. These actions include what cognitive psychologists call "implicit memory" which are memories we retrieve without being aware that we are having a memory. An example is remembering how to ride a bicycle, how to turn a doorknob, or drive a car. In order to do these things, we have to unconsciously access our memories of how to perform those activities. Other activities performed by the unconscious mind include thoughts, judgments, and actions we take but are consciously unaware of why we take them. We can look to our unconscious mind as the source of our automatic reactions and thoughts, our symbolic dreams, and forgotten memories which surface at key points in time.

This recognition of a different level of consciousness has been shared by many ancient cultures, including the Egyptians, Hebrews, and Hindus. References to the unconscious mind can be found in the writings of some Medieval Christians and Renaissance philosophers while more recognition of this principle was more fully explored by such German philosophers as Schopenhauer, Nietzsche, and Hegel. These great thinkers were certain that our behavior is motivated by more than just our conscious understanding of the world. Our thoughts and behaviors are often directed by the portions of our mind outside of our own awareness.

An easy way to explain how the conscious mind and the unconscious mind work together is to use the analogy of a ship. On this ship your conscious mind is the captain. The captain gives the orders directing where the ship goes and when it is to return. The unconscious mind represents the crew on the ship. The crew follows the orders of the captain and continues to perform their duties based on these orders. The ship continues to sail the waters as long as the orders the crew is given do not change.

The orders the crew received are not judged by the crew. If the captain gave orders to sail a certain direction based on an environmental factor, like a storm, the crew would willingly obey orders without question. The problem arises when the captain suddenly one day attempts to change the course of the ship. Even though the captain has given a new order, the crew is accustomed to the old route and old orders. This results in the crew ignoring the captain's directives. No matter what the captain does, the crew continues to obey the old orders. Sometimes these orders were given many, many years ago and are no longer pertinent, yet the crew will still follow these outdated orders.

This conflict was clear in a client whom I will call David. David was about sixty years old and had been fighting to lose weight for most of his life. He was physically obese, and his doctor warned him that he was going to have a heart attack if he did not immediately lose weight. David told me he had tried to lose weight for many years. He would start an exercise program and then fall off his schedule. He tried every diet he learned about and then would stop after a few weeks. He was concerned for his health while also feeling ashamed and angry at himself for not having more will power. He told me his biggest problem was snacking at night when he became anxious. He found that snacking on food helped him relax. David had no idea why he felt anxious since, other than his weight, everything else in his life was going well.

I decided to work with David using a process that helps clients quickly enter a mild trance state where they can circumvent their conscious minds and directly enter the realm of the unconscious. When clients are in this realm, they can swiftly clear issues which have been affecting their lives by blocking their emotional and spiritual development. In our sessions we rapidly got to the root of David's problem. When David was eleven years old, he was sexually assaulted. While he was helping a man clean the church his family attended, the man assaulted him. This event was obviously physically and emotional traumatic for David. He remembered being alone that night in his room after the attack and literally shaking with fear. He told no one about this incident because he was told by the man who assaulted him that no one would believe David. In his desire to instantly have some feeling of calm during the after effect of his ordeal, David reached out for some sugary snack cakes. He enjoyed the taste, and the cakes made him feel a little better for a little while. He continued to reach for junk food over the next week when he started to feel the beginning signs of discomfort due to the horribly traumatic event.

Now at sixty years old, David had stopped consciously thinking about his sexual assault. He rarely thought about it at all. However, his unconscious mind had not forgotten. It was

91

still playing a pattern which had developed over the past forty-nine years. His unconscious mind had received the command to eat when feelings of fear appeared and David was still playing this program in his mind. Anytime he felt a little anxious he reached for food. His conscious mind, the captain, had ordered his unconscious mind, the crew, to behave differently, but the crew mutinied and continued to follow the orders they were accustomed to following. The crew wanted to feel better, and eating was the only way they knew how to do it.

In our sessions, we worked through the emotional block caused by the assault. We then cleared up any illogical beliefs he had been carrying about himself. When we were done with our work, he told me he felt like a different person. He told me he felt so much lighter in his body. His conscious and unconscious minds were now working together without fear or negative judgment. He had dropped the emotional weight he had been carrying and was better able to deal with the physical weight he wanted to lose. Four weeks later he told me he had already lost nearly fourteen pounds with very little exercise. He realized he did not feel the need to snack any more. He was now more relaxed and focused on achieving his weight loss goal. By accessing his unconscious realm, he was able to free himself from his pattern of turning to food as the only way to deal with anxiety and stress.

Sigmund Freud, the father of psychotherapy, was one of the first in the West to popularize the concept of the unconscious mind. Freud believed that much of our dysfunctional patterns of behavior are rooted in our unconscious minds. Freud viewed the unconscious as a container of the emotions, thoughts, biological drives, and memories that are outside the awareness of our conscious mind. To Freud, most of the things in the container are objectionable or unsettling, such as past trauma, anxiety and emotional pain. According to Freud, the unconscious continues to influence our behavior and experience, even though we are unaware of these underlying influences.

Freud believed the unconscious mind works to maintain the homeostasis of our inner world by hiding the thoughts which we perceive as unacceptable, threatening or challenging to our inner most beliefs or sense of self. The unconscious will then project these thoughts outside of our self. We will then experience these outwardly projected thoughts as if they are not connected to ourselves. Freud felt the intensity and the breadth of the information concealed from us often is displaced onto other people and the world outside of us.

Our unconscious thoughts and beliefs are projected into the world whether they are good or bad, whether they work for us or whether they work against us. If we have intense mental absorption of a particular thought, this thought will often be projected out onto the outside world. If we believe the world is a dangerous place, our unconscious will only give us a perception of the world that will support this unconscious belief and mirror back situations that gives us "proof" to confirm to ourselves that the world is indeed dangerous. Essentially all that is projected out to the world will be reflected back to our unconscious mind unmodified.

"Our life always expresses the result of our dominant thoughts." - **Soren Kierkegaard**

One way to think about this is to imagine you had been born with sunglasses on. You never knew you had sunglasses on so you never took them off. You wore the sunglasses every day and every night. You saw the same world as everyone else only your view of the world was a little darker. No matter what time of day you looked out, it was always a little darker than other people's experience of looking outside. You have never known anything was different about wearing sunglasses so you continue to wear them without any conscious awareness. One day you discover that you have been wearing those sunglasses, and you decide to take them off. You are totally unprepared for how different the world looks! The sunset you saw before was nice but the one you look at now without the sunglasses is breathtaking with vibrant and intense colors. Our awareness of our unconscious mind can transform our day to day experiences.

If this is the case, why doesn't everyone throw off their sunglasses and see the world in a healthier and happier way? The reason is that those sunglasses are still unconsciously worn. They can't take the sunglasses off because they are unaware that they even exist, sometimes even after they have been told! Essentially, the unconscious mind is the invisible filter through which you see the world. You never are fully aware of this filter, but yet it exists and filters everything you see. If your filter is filled with the feelings of worthlessness and mistrust, you will approach relationships differently than if your filter contained self-love and self-acceptance.

We believe the world is outside of ourselves due to the way we filter incoming information. This information originates with our five senses (visual, auditory, kinesthetic, gustatory and olfactory). This sensory information is gathered from the outside world. We depend on these senses to obtain information about the external world. We take in this information through neurological sense receptors. These actions occur in the realm of our brain's neural connections.

We are not aware of all the information because our unconscious minds will filter out any information that does not correspond to our unconscious beliefs about ourselves and the world around us. Some information is accepted but only because it conforms to the belief structure of our unconscious minds. Anything that does not fit the criteria laid down by the unconscious is often kicked out and therefore never enters our awareness.

This filtering of information is what generates our sense of Self. Who we think we are may be based more on what information we unconsciously consume than who we really are. The generation of our Self is a dynamic process constantly reinforced until something happens and we become aware of information that was previously held outside of our conscious minds. In order to maintain our unconscious beliefs, we ensure that we only accept information that validates those beliefs. If information is the opposite of our beliefs, often we will not notice that specific information. This is another unconscious process. The unconscious mind tries to maintain the same pattern of belief it has held for a long time. It is again the ship's crew trying to follow the old, familiar route. If we hear or see any information that challenges our deep held beliefs about our Self we often just plain ignore it. Cognitive therapists call this "selective perception."

For example, imagine that a man who has a very racist outlook on life is watching the nightly news. This man does not like anyone who has a darker skin color than him. As he is watching the local news, there are several stories about crimes committed in the area with accompanying pictures of the perpetrators. Over the course of the news story the screen flashes pictures of three Caucasian males and three African-American males. After seeing all of these pictures, the man then thinks to himself, "I knew black guys were criminals." He has reinforced his ignorant belief by perceiving only the pictures of the African-American men. He unconsciously deleted any mental reference to the three men who were the same color as he.

This happens all the time in the way we see the world. We form sweeping generalizations, and we base it upon limited information. We reinforce this information by deleting anything that disagrees with our deep held beliefs, and our initial experiences often create beliefs that limit us. Certain experiences, particularly early in our lives, can set the ground work for future unconscious reactions to similar situations. As a result of the earlier experience, we frequently expect the same outcomes that we received earlier. This creates a limited way of interacting with our world. Thus, the reality we experience is based on our own projections and the expectations we have developed about these projections.

This process happens so often that it becomes a habit as it is automatic and completely unknown to us. It is difficult to be aware of this process because it is this very process that determines what information we access. If a woman believes that she is ugly when in reality she is very beautiful, she will often continue to filter out any information that does not confirm her belief that she is ugly. She will politely accept a compliment, but down deep she will not truly appreciate the message of the compliment since it does not match her unconscious belief. When she thinks about her looks she will only recall the negative messages and things that confirm her ugliness. The compliments on her beauty have been filtered out of her awareness, and she may not even remember any compliments until someone points them out to her.

We process this incoming information based on the way our unconscious mind chooses to reinforce and retain its present structure of experience. The majority of what we perceive may be misperceptions based on this process of projection and reflection. This is also how we unconsciously seek to reduce our anxiety, anger and guilt. Believing the causes of these emotions are outside ourselves, we can instead look to other sources to blame. Rather than bringing our awareness to these uncomfortable feelings, we instead view the causes of our problems as other people or situations that have little to do with the way we live our lives. As a result, we feel helpless and victimized.

These mistaken notions cause us to believe we have no power to change our circumstances or our attitudes. As long as people are unaware of what they project and what is reflected back, they will feel powerless and trapped in a life of mental slavery. This illusion will seem very real until exploration of the unconscious mind begins. As soon as a people begin to examine and challenge their unconscious beliefs, they find that a fog lifts and the light of awakening begins to pour in. As we dig deep and discover how our thinking developed, we realize we have options and can challenge the limited thinking which has kept us psychological immobilized. When this happens, our fear, anxiety and guilt diminishes, and we start living a life of our own choosing. We can open up to magical possibilities that have been there waiting for us.

Researchers have found that our perceptions can have an impact on how our DNA responds. The field of epigenetics, which focuses on how the interactions with the environment can change how our genes respond, gives us insight into how our unconscious mind and bodily processes can affect our quality of life. Genes, which are composed of DNA, carry instructions on how to create proteins which allow our bodies to develop and to function. Often our environments create certain experiences and literally change the amount and the quality of the phenotype, which is the observable characteristic of the gene.

To be as simple as possible, there are small molecules separate from DNA which enable the interaction between the environment and genes. This process is called "methylation", and it has the capacity to create changes in how our genes function. This process can literally start or stop the DNA transcription process, which can alter the synthesizing of proteins and can even add different molecules to the proteins after the synthesis has finished.

Now you may be asking yourself what all this jargon has to do with our thoughts and beliefs. To really get a real world understanding, let's use an example. Imagine a child who has spent his life in a world of violence and poverty. The child's family has had to deal with a lack of food and safety. The child has had little experience of comfort and peace during his formative years. As a result of the child's experiences of violence and poverty, his perception of the environment is that it is very dangerous. This perception creates a neurochemical reaction which leads to a chronic stress response in the child. As a result of this perception, a substance known as brain derived neurotrophic factor (BDNF), which is essential to creating new neurons and neural connections in the brain, is inhibited. This causes an epigenetic mechanism that instructs the genes to slow down its production of BDNF. The slowing down of the production of BDNF can lead to long term mental and physical health issues. If the child continues to perceive his environment as very dangerous (even if he has grown up and moved to a better environment), then it is likely that the gene controlling the creation of new neurons and neural connections will still be inhibited.

When we apply this information to our own lives, we find that there is no separation between the object (what is

99

happening outside you) and the observer (what is happening inside you). If the observer determines the outcome, then it is we who determine how we experience our lives. We are not merely observers seeing what is outside us, but instead, we are participants with what we observe. The outcome can change when we become our own observer. By observing our own minds, we can change them, and this will, in turn, change the way we think, feel, and act in the future.

We are not our thoughts

Many of the unconscious thoughts and beliefs we have about ourselves and the world around us came from our earlier experiences. In many of these experiences we were children who were trying to make sense of this often confusing world. The very actions and reactions that served us in staying safe and getting our basic needs met as children may not serve us in our adult lives. However, in spite of this we often react in those old habitual ways. Our minds are capable adapting to a variety of environments. We can learn to adapt to unhealthy environments in ways which allow us to survive and to make sense of what is occurring to us. The ability to adapt may indeed assist us in surviving in the short term, but later it can block our physical, emotional and spiritual development.

As we grow, we may find ourselves stuck at a certain level of emotional development and reacting to the world in dysfunctional ways. We may be afraid to take chances on living our dreams or on connecting with others. This is not due to what is actually happening to us now but is fear based on old, outdated modes of thought. Unconscious thinking such as "The world is always dangerous," "I am not strong enough to survive," "Things never work out for me," or "I never have enough," limit our health and happiness and keep us frozen in a less than empowered existence.

Many people are trapped in limited and fearful ways of thinking about themselves. They accept these unconscious thought processes and believe they are their thoughts. Their thoughts and beliefs about the world have become their identities. Unfortunately, they identify themselves not with who they really are, but with a set of mental habits. These habits rule their lives and convince them that they have no choice in how to respond to their environment. These seemingly automatic ways of interacting with the environment were not in place at birth. It is through experience that brains have been shaped to respond in such consistent ways. This is the foundation of a theory in neuroscience called Hebb's rule.

Introduced in 1949 by Canadian psychologist Donald Hebb, the basic idea of Hebb's rule is that neurons, which fire together, will build stronger connections that aids in stabilization. A common phrase used when discussing this theory is "neurons that fire together, wire together". On the other hand, neurons which do not fire together are not able to stabilize and are ultimately removed. If the neurons do not fire and wire together, then over time all previous connections will disappear. The repeated stimulation of a specific neural pathway will solidify the connections within that pathway.

What this means to us is that when we repeatedly think in a different way, our brain can physically change. The firing of your neurons will shift when you change the things you focus on. The changes observed by the mind will bring about changes in the flow of neurochemical activity. If you focus on fearful things, those images and emotions will become solidified in your unconscious mind. If, however, you focus on empowering possibilities, in time your unconscious mind will be guided in that direction.

It was once a common belief that our brains was structurally "fixed" after we became adults. Due to the discovery of something called "neuroplasticity" we find that by intentionally focusing on specific emotions and ideas, we can create physical changes in the structuring of our brains. This is an amazing concept! The mind, which I will define as activity created by the brain, can cause changes in the brain to change by consciously choosing what to pay attention to. For example, if you are feeling stressed due to a situation at work, spending time paying attention to thoughts about positive outcomes you can adjust the level of stress hormones which are released into your body. This allows you to relax. When you decide to change your mind, your brain changes, and in turn your experience of the world changes. These new findings in neuroscience give credence to the ancient wisdom of many different cultures that the quality of our lives is determined by the quality of our thoughts. .

Habitual thought patterns transform our brains. The

neural connections created by our intense, concentration on a thought can activate a substantial number of neurons. As a result of this focus, these connections are solidified, and habits are strengthened at the unconscious level. It is by conscious attention that we can rewire our brains. If our attention is focused on empowering beliefs, we strengthen those connections. And in the same manner, the more we focus on negative beliefs the more we stabilize those neural pathways. It is really up to us how we want our brains to work.

This can be equated to a well-worn path in the forest. If every day we walk on one specific path, then that path will continue to become more worn and will appear to be the only path. However, if we decide to create other paths, we may be surprised how many other paths we have to get through the forest. The only way to make a new path more accessible is to walk on it as often as possible to ensure it becomes deeply worn. As we do this, we may notice the old path has begun to sprout weeds so we can barely see it. From that point on we will automatically take our new path.

"Our virtues are habits, as much as our vices. Our lives are but a mass of habits." -**William James**

By consciously focusing on the reality we wish to create, we use our brain's natural purpose of scanning our environment and adjust the scanning power to include new information that will bring our desires to life. We must begin to view our thoughts, not as our fixed identity, but rather as tools that can work for us only when we take charge of them.

"Take up one idea. Make that one idea your life - think of it, dream of it, live on that idea. Let the brain, muscles, nerves, every part of your body, be full of that idea, and just leave every other idea alone. This is the way to success. That is the way great spiritual giants are produced." -Swami Vivekananda

We are capable of determining of not only what thoughts we have, but also changing the ones that inhibit us. We can choose what thoughts we want to keep and what thoughts we want to reject. Since the observations we have about the world are constructions of our own minds, we can stop feeling helpless, victimized and fearful. These constructions can be torn down and rebuilt with peaceful, loving and empowering structures. This is one of the greatest psychological discoveries of all time. It is very simple in concept, but is so very profound. We have a choice in what we project into our world. We may have believed we were observers of what develops around us, but now we know the very thing we are watching is ourselves. We all have the potential to become more aware of why we think what we think, and how to change the way we experience life. In adjusting our thinking, we create a magical mind which can endow us with more contentment, happiness and joy as we navigate this incredible world we inhabit.

CHAPTER 3: THE MAGIC OF DREAMS

Every night when we close our eyes to sleep we enter into a magical world. We experience without limitations. When we are dreaming we go deeply inside our unconscious minds and interact with places which may be foreign to our conscious minds. We gain access to a place where parts of us previously unknown come intensely and vividly into our awareness. If we are open to our dream world, it is quite possible there are messages waiting that we need to hear in order to move our lives toward magical encounters.

"The dream is a little hidden door in the innermost and most secret resources of the psyche." – **C.G. Jung**

Dreams have always fascinated human kind. From the earliest civilizations there is evidence that nighttime dreams have great power and contain important information that we need to heed. Dreams have been viewed as a source of wisdom and guidance from other sources and were a spiritual event. Ancient cultures dating as far back as the Sumerians, Babylonians, Assyrians and Egyptians believed that dreams contain great meaning and can have a major impact on our waking lives. These cultures viewed dreams as the voice of one's soul and the soul's connection to higher powers.

Many traditions held that dreaming was a process of

connecting to the divine source from which all things emanate since our souls are not burdened by the limitation of the five senses. Further, these traditions believed we are able to tune in directly to the divine. Actively working with dreams was accepted as a spiritual practice of great power and was used for everything from understanding day to day conflicts, to divination, to further exploring the deepest levels of our psyche. Working with dreams is a method of accessing inner resources from which esoteric insights can be obtained and then utilized for personal growth. Using these inner resources and insights can be a way to better align us with our purpose in life.

Most of the religions in the world generally agree that some dreams contain revelations from the divine. In the Greco-Roman period, it was believed that dreams were created and sent directly by the gods. Plato believed, much like later depth psychologists, that our desires emerge and seek realization in our dreams. Many cultures have long believed that the soul is released from the confines of the body during sleep, and dreams are our excursions through the spirit world.

The content of dreams has usually been seen as a symbolic perspective. Understanding these symbols and metaphors were crucial in tapping into the healing power of the dream which could grant insight to dreamers, aiding in the journey toward wholeness. Shamans have traditionally used dreams to obtain information to heal people. They also have viewed dreams as the call to become a shaman. The information contained in a dream was regarded as sacred and to be used with the highest reverence.

Even though some of our dreams appear nonsensical, we are hard pressed not to find certain dreams containing important symbolic information which, if properly examined, may have a crucial impact on our waking lives. Carl Jung believed that our dreams examine our conscious attitudes since our conscious defenses, used for coping with our problems, are not available when we enter the sleeping world of the unconscious mind. Intense dreams can bring a greater awareness of the unconscious into being. These special dreams are how our unconscious thoughts, feelings and beliefs enter into our waking state. These dreams bring an expansion of awareness about ourselves and others and often give us a new perspective on how we view our lives.

Jung himself consulted his dreams regularly, and due to one of his dreams he had a major breakthrough about the depth of the unconscious mind. Jung dreamed he came to a large house. Once inside the house, he noticed there were multiple levels in the house. He decided to go down to the next level of the house. On the next level, he found a large, dark hall with a variety of furnishings from the medieval time period. He decided to go down another level. Here there was a vaulted Roman cellar. Jung looked down and saw in the floor a large stone slab with an iron ring in it. He pulled the iron ring which opened the slab to reveal a dark, tunnel. This tunnel led Jung down into an ancient cave. In the cave, Jung saw a variety of old broken pots and human bones. As he stood in the cave he felt a sense of awe of the antiquity of the items.

Upon waking from this dream, Jung had an insight about the nature of the unconscious. He believed that this dream had directed him to his concept of the "collective unconscious." Jung theorized that there is a part of our unconscious which contains a collection of symbols which are shared by every human. These universal symbols are cross cultural and possibly genetic in every human being and unconsciously shared across humanity. These symbols often influence how we interact and what actions we take when activated in our minds. Jung believed the symbols often appeared in dreams. By being open to his dreams, Jung had an insight which would change the nature of how people perceived the unconscious mind.

Our dreams can warn us when we are off course in our lives. They can also nurture us and reassure us when we are going through difficult times. Our dreams can alert us to new opportunities and strengthen our resolve to follow our purpose and to achieve our goals. By paying attention to the unconscious signals found in our dreams, we become more aware of a much deeper spiritual connection to the world around us. Dreams can give us a glimpse of what our deepest desires are and direct us in finding them. A repetitive dream of playing at a grandparents' home may indicate that we long for the freedom, spontaneity and creativity which we used to embody during that time. It could also let us know how we lost that part of our identity and energy.

Many of today's brain researchers and psychologists have little place for dreaming as a magical or spiritual process. Dreams are seen as random fluctuations of neurons which stimulated old patterns obtained during our waking lives. Even in most modern psychotherapies, dreams contribute little to the therapy process since the role of the unconscious is often overlooked or ignored. I believe dreams can tell us much about how to live our lives more effectively and more aligned with nature if only we open our minds to this possibility. If many of the answers to life's mysteries are already inside our unconscious mind, our dreams are one of the gateways to those answers.

Dreams can seem so odd that, even though we may intuitively know there is a message for us in the dream, it can be difficult to find any meaning. Every now and then we have a dream that holds a meaning that is so obvious to us that it shakes us to the core. Often, however, a dream gives us many secrets while the secrets hide in plain sight. What we think we know about our dreams may be just scratching the surface. By taking time to reflect on our dreams, we can allow insights from the unconscious to eventually surface. Over my year of living magically, I regularly paid a great deal of attention to what my dreams were relaying to me. I found that many times I would gain deep insights by just allowing my mind to freely think about a dream which I had experienced the previous night. In order to get the most out of our dreams, we must be open to what information our unconscious mind gives us, even if at first it appears nonsensical.

It is crucial to have a pen and pad near your bed when you begin investigating the unconscious world of your dreams. We all have had the experience of a vivid dream and remembering all the details of it for a few moments after waking. The details eventually drift away as our minds becomes more awake, and we are left wondering what the dream was about which moved us so much. By having a pen and pad near the bed, we can instantly write down the dream without fear of losing the details of the dream to the oncoming activity of the day. I also believe that by writing down the dream, we are giving our unconscious mind a signal that we are open to the messages it sends us. When we let our unconscious mind know that we are receptive to what it brings us, we are more likely to receive more of what it has to give. In addition to your magical life journal, you also want to have a journal just for your dreams. Doing this invites in all sorts of magical experiences in the nocturnal world.

A dream is unfiltered emotional data from our inner world. It can come to us in symbols we don't initially understand, however, with proper reflection, we can learn much from it. I remember having a dream when I was going through my divorce which, at first, seemed to have an obvious meaning, but on deeper reflection it said much more than I realized. I dreamed that I was standing on the banks of a large lake with marshes around it. My wife and stepdaughter stood behind me. All of a sudden large, frightening alligators began to come out of the lake to attack us. I jumped in front of my wife and stepdaughter to protect them and picked up a large stick which was lying on the ground. I began striking at the alligators to keep them away from my family. The alligators emerged from the lake one at a time and would withdraw after I struck at them, only to return a moment later.

As this frightening battle continued, a bus drove up behind us. The bus opened its doors, and my wife and stepdaughter got on the bus. The doors closed, and the bus drove away leaving me to fight the alligators by myself. I remember watching in horror as the bus drove off, wondering where my wife and stepdaughter had gone and what I was to do with the onslaught of the alligators. I awoke with a start and was surprised how much that dream affected me. For the rest of the day I was felt a bit off due to the dream.

The next day I sat quietly and thought about what the dream meant to me. I certainly could see the aspect of being abandoned by my family very clearly. I was aware that when things got tough in life, I seemed to be the one who had to deal with them. I could understand my feelings of abandonment and the lack of support that was symbolically projected into the dream. All of a sudden, a question came from the back of my mind, "What was the meaning of the bus in the dream?" My first thought was that it was just a random image used to take my family away from the alligators. My inner self was not so sure this was true.

I continued to sit quietly and think about the bus in the dream. I let my imagination freely flow and decided that I would ask the bus what was its purpose. I imagined the scene of the dream again, and this time, I turned and asked the bus why it was taking away my family. The bus did not directly talk to me, but a feeling came which gave me the answer to my question. The bus was not there to hurt me by taking away my family. It was there to help me by making sure my family was safe. It let me know that my family was not strong enough to deal with what was going on so they had to run away. They loved me, but they did not have the resolve I had to fight the alligators. The bus let me know that they just weren't ready to fight with me. They had to grow stronger before they could face the dangers of the lake.

The insight in the dream then hit me hard. My wife and stepdaughter couldn't give me what they didn't have. I had wanted love and acceptance from them, particularly my wife, and yet they did not have it to give since they had not given themselves love and acceptance. I wanted support and compassion, but they did not have it to give me. I realized that we cannot give anyone anything that we don't have for ourselves. I had wanted things from my family which they were not able to give me at this time in their lives. The bus had come to take them because they would have been eaten by the alligators if they stayed. I was strong enough to fight the alligators so the bus left me to deal with them.

When I became aware of this insight, I began to cry. Although I still had anger toward my wife for leaving, I now had empathy for what she was feeling. I now understood that, in spite of my doing everything I could to the best of my ability, I could never fully receive what I wanted from her until she was able to find it within herself. In some ways she showed great courage in leaving the relationship since even though she loved me, she realized that she couldn't give me the partner I needed at that time. The dream had revealed a layer of my situation that I needed to know but could not consciously experience due to the emotional pain of being abandoned. The insight from the dream marked a turning

113

point in my healing.

The imagery in dreams can be strange and sometimes even frightening. Nightmares are dreams that shake us to our core. These types of dreams demand that our conscious mind take notice of them. We remember these dreams more easily than others due to their intensity and because our fight or flight responses become active while we sleep. Some dream experts believe that nightmares of being chased by monsters and demons appear to let the dreamer know that there is some inescapable aspect of life which he or she may be avoiding.

I remember talking with a college student who had frequent nightmares of a huge snarling beast chasing her down a long corridor. The dream ended with the student being cornered, and the beast jumping to attack. The student would then wake up in full panic mode and wonder why she continued having such a horrifying dream. In our discussions, it turned out that she was extremely stressed in her academics. She had to pass an extremely difficult class or she would be unable to enter a specific program. This program led to a career which she had wanted to do since she was a child and much was riding on passing the tough class. She had her insight about the dream when she told me she felt the class was going to "eat her alive." When she saw that her anxiety about passing the class was showing up in her dream, she felt a sense of relief knowing that once the class was over she would be saying goodbye to the terrible beast that chased her. She passed the class, got into her program, and reported no more beasts in dreamtime.

There may be some part of a person which seems to be unsettling to the conscious mind, and the only way the unconscious can alert the dreamer is through the nightmare. Jung called the part, "the shadow" and it can appear frightening to our conscious minds. The qualities of "the shadow" are so far removed from the conscious sense of self that it can appear scary. We often project "the shadow" onto others rather than examine and own it ourselves. The power in "the shadow" is so great that it demands to be acknowledged and will seek the acknowledgement in the symbolic nature of our dreams. If we repeatedly experience a dream in which we are attacked by an unseen force, we may need to examine what part of our Self may be attacking something or someone. It may be that we are the ones who, in the non-dreaming world, are attacking an idea, a situation or a person. This is too hard for our sense of self to acknowledge. And as a result will be projected as an unseen force in our dreams which wreaks havoc and instills fear in us.

I remember talking with a man who had a recurring dream of walking through a very large house and finding a very aggressive dog in each room. Each room he entered the dog would attack him until he was able to leave the room. When he went into another room a different dog was waiting to attack him. This dream was obviously disconcerting to him, and he was puzzled by why he continued to have it. One day it dawned on him that he was treating his employees the way the dogs in the large house were treating him. He was very difficult to work with since he believed he had to be tough to get respect form his employees. He was aggressive with them, and this caused much hardship for them and for himself. He realized that the part of him that attacked was much like the dogs because the only reason the dogs attacked was they felt they were in danger. This led to his working on his fear of losing control in the work place. In time his bark and bite decreased, and his employees could begin to relax. He also ceased dreaming of large houses with dogs in them. His "shadow" made an appearance in his dream and helped him to see himself in a more realistic light.

If dreams hold access to our unconscious, we may want to consider actively working with our dreams to discover insights and ideas which can help us in living magical lives. Throughout the centuries, working with dreams has been an accepted practice in learning about the natural world. Greek philosophers such as Pythagoras and Parmenides gave much validity to the unseen world of dreams. They participated in elaborate rituals to access the dream world for such diverse reasons as learning, prophecy, and healing. In the Old Testament there are many stories of dreams, particularly Joseph who decoded dreams for the Pharaohs. The ancients believed in the inner wisdom of the unconscious mind. We have the same ability to investigate our dream world. Using the following exercise, see what magical things may occur when you begin working with your dreams.

Exercise – Incubating Your Dream

Step 1: Choose a night when you are sure that your sleep will not be interrupted. Pick a night in which the next morning will not be rushed with activities so that you can take your time arising.

Step 2: Right before you lay down to sleep, write down in your journal any important emotional aspects that occurred during your day. Write down anything which claimed your attention (good and bad). Write down any small details about these events.

Step 3: After writing down all the emotional aspects of your day, put the entire situation into a short phrase. For example, if you are having a hard time with a coworker named Jim and have written down all the problems you are having with him, you might write the phrase, "Discover a way to work peacefully with Jim."

Step 4: Now that you have your short phrase, repeat it to yourself many times as you meditate on the outcome you want to have.

Step 5: Release the phrase along with any associate images with the phrase and allow yourself to drift off to sleep.

Step 6: Immediately upon waking, record any dreams you had. If you do not recall any dreams, record what emotions and sensations you are feeling in the moment.

Step 7: Take time to reflect on what you wrote. Write down answers to the following questions: What is the most vivid part of the dream? Are there any abrupt shifts in the setting or characters in the dream? What are the strangest elements of the dream? How am I like this dream?

Step 8: When you have thoroughly examined the dream and written down the answers to the previous questions, set the dream aside and begin to look for things in your daily life that remind you of your dream. Notice signs from the unconscious that remind you of your dream. Pay attention to new ideas and feelings which trigger memories of the dream you had. After three weeks look back over the situation and see what changes have taken place.

When we purposefully incubate the dream, we sow the seeds for direct contact with the unconscious mind. We are able to set the stage to obtain inspired information which can assist us when faced by challenges. Our dream world can become our ally if we allow and accept what it gives us. Often we will not like our dreams, but if we take the time to allow the unconscious content of the dream to unfold, we may find much value in what we have been given.

Over my year of living magically, I used this exercise fairly regularly and gained many insights about myself and my situation. I also began to appreciate my dreams more. When I put the insights I had gained from my dreams into practical action, I routinely found that I moved forward in my life in surprising ways. I have come to think of my dreams as an internal guidance system which lets me know I am off course in my life. It helps me in redirecting myself to get back on course. I have learned that when my unconscious mind works together with my conscious mind, magical things can happen. By allowing ourselves to become more open to our dreams, we gain access to the most mysterious thing in the world: our own true selves.

CHAPTER 4: CREATING MAGICAL SPACE

The space we daily occupy can be very important to our mental health. If we spend much time in a specific place, then we want to feel comfortable and inspired in that particular space. Often we do not pay attention to what surrounds us in our homes or offices. Even though these places may be decorated in the latest styles, they still may not be arranged in a manner that causes us to feel at ease and full of possibility. If our space does not encourage us to tap into our magical side, then it is a space that we need to change.

Awareness of our space is nothing new. Our ancestors believed that certain spaces were important to revere and protect. They believed that spending time in those places aided them in accessing their inner self and connecting more deeply with nature. As we are interconnected with nature, it is natural for us to feel there are specific places that cause shifts in our thoughts and emotions. These places could be tied to our past, such as where we grew up or where we had positive or negative life changes. There are also special sacred places in the world where just by being there we can feel a change in our awareness and a decrease in our stress. These particular places draw people so that they can experience the power of the place.

It has been conjectured that sacred places are connected to the energy of the Earth and these places can affect consciousness. Many believe these places had a particular form of energy that is activated when people enter them. Many of the ancient temples were designed to mark specific changes in the seasons and movements of the moon and sun. In the distant past, people would come to sacred sites on specific dates to ritually walk in a circular fashion around the holy site. This circular pattern often represented the movement of the sun throughout the day or the season. The ritual of circling the site represented the influence of the sun on daily life. Sometimes these rituals ended with walking in the opposite direction. This was an attempt to undo the earlier solar action so that the land remained balanced energetically. These rituals were symbolic actions used to create changes in the awareness of the person or group acting them out. The space was a place for the acting out of a myth which helped people make sense of the natural world around them.

"Myths are best seen as narrative patterns of consciousness that underlie the universe of our experience, not as accounts within that universe." **– John Michael Greer**

Some researchers assume that the type of stones used at these places of power may have qualities which aid in the transformation of one's consciousness since these places were used for healing physical and emotional issues. Like the people of the past, we need to consider how our surroundings can affect our mental and emotional well-being. When we consciously adjust our environment to reflect our inner world, we can create a place which reinforces positive mood and possibility thinking.

Magicians during medieval times believed that the space for creating spells was just as important as the spell they wished to create. If they created a spell in an environment that ran counter to the results they wanted, then they believed the outcomes would be meager at best. There are accounts of magicians clearing a space of negativity so that they could perform their magical rituals. It was not uncommon for a magician to have a space specifically set aside for only the performance of magical rituals so that the space would not be polluted by negative energy.

All of this speaks to the importance we place on our own space. If our living space is uncomfortable, we may have problems feeling creative and rested. If our work space is sterile and cold, we may find that our energy to perform work becomes uninspired. All of us have been in an environment that caused us to feel less than resourceful. It may have been that the space was not a match for us. It did not make us feel welcome or comfortable. It did not give us a secure feeling which we could build upon. I have seen this in different medical offices. One office is very warm and inviting and the other is cold and barren. Even though both doctors in each office are competent and caring, the patient's feeling toward seeing the doctor, and indirectly getting better, may be influenced by the space the doctor is presenting.

Certain neighborhoods can cause us to feel less than comfortable even though the outward appearance is one of harmony and peace. Even if we don't see a place sometimes we can feel inside ourselves the lack of harmony which emanates from the area. I remember driving home late one evening from being out of town. I decided to take a short cut through the county I lived which is an economically desperate area. There have been generations of poverty in the area since the old factories closed long ago. My wife was lying back in the front seat with her eyes closed. She had no idea what area we were driving through. All of a sudden she opens her eyes and, without sitting up in her seat to see anything, she says to me, "This place feels bad to me." I asked what she meant. She told me that she felt the area was causing her to feel a sense of despair. I was surprised but said nothing else. As soon as we exited the area my wife, with her eyes still closed and lying back in the seat, told me, "This feels better now". She had for some reason tuned into the space around her and had physically sensed the sad conditions the residents inhabited.

If we know that our space can affect us so much then we need to consciously choose what kind of space we would like to inhabit. We may not be able to choose the neighborhood we presently live in but we can choose how we arrange our inner lodging. Sometimes something as simple as a small change in the color in a room can charge the area with a totally different feeling. Creating a magical life also involves creating an environment in which magic can occur. It can be tough to create a magical life if the majority of our time is spent in uninspiring spaces. It is not out of the ordinary for some people to take a break from work and sit outside. They return with a brilliant insight which never

123

occurred to them stuck in an office. Decide that, starting today, you want to have a magical space that is all yours. It does not matter if it is at home or work or outside. As long as it makes you feel alive and creative then the space is magical for you.

Being out in nature gives us plenty of opportunities to find magical spaces. When I visited my local state park, I went to a certain place off the beaten path (where most magical places reside). I sat there quietly and undisturbed while listening to the sounds of the flowing water of the creek and the songs of the birds sitting in the trees. This space not only gave me solitude, it also gave me a feeling of deep connection to the earth. I found that when I spent time in my special place in the park, I returned rejuvenated to take on any upcoming tasks.

Magical spaces are there for us so that we can reflect on our lives and take time to recharge. Taking retreats in scenic locations may be an attempt by us to connect with the magic of the natural landscape and gain perspective on our lives. I knew a woman who spent the majority of her time in her garden which she viewed as a magical place. She told me she liked to imagine that she had "garden fairies" that helped her create such a beautiful, peaceful place. Her laughter and enjoyment digging in the dirt created a place where, no matter what was going on in her life, she always had a space to go which transported her to a place of serenity.

I knew a man who was an architect and had built a small structure in his backyard where he would retreat when he needed to feel inspired. Inside the structure he had paintings and pictures of people and places which caused him to feel inspired. He had painted the inside of the structure in colors which helped him to relax. He installed a small stereo system on which he played soft, soothing music. He went to this structure several times a week. His wife knew to leave him alone while he was inside his structure because he was creating new things in his mind. He would return to the evening dinner table with a new found energy which had not possessed until he went to his magical space in the backyard. His wife eventually asked if she could go sit in his space when he was not using it, and he agreed. She also found great comfort in the space and would take her needlepoint work so that she could enjoy her hobby in solitude and peace.

It is not uncommon in ancient stories to read of people taking journeys to find magical places. The forest is often the destination when the characters in the stories are inspired to seek out unknown, magical landscapes. Joseph Campbell details the common threads in most ancient myths in what he called, "The Hero's Journey." All of the characters in the hero's journey had to leave the place which was familiar to them in order to venture into a mysterious world and gain what they sought. In the end, maybe all of them were really seeking a magical space that they could call their own.

In my home I have a certain chair I sit in when I enjoy my early morning coffee. It is by the window and surrounded by several beautiful plants. As I quietly drink my coffee and allow my mind to wander, I often come up with wonderful business or personal ideas. I decided sit in that chair only when I want to allow my mind to ride the flow of creativity. Most every morning I get to enjoy a magical space that is as simple as an old recliner by a window. I find that when I want to solve a problem or come up with a new idea, the chair by the window is the place I seek out. I meditate and contemplate in that chair and I can enter a state of relaxation and tranquility. It also is a place in which I can focus more easily when making decisions which I do not need to take lightly.

That space in my home has become magical to me. It helped me to move through places I felt stuck over the year. The space which gives me such wonderful feelings adheres to the concept of classical conditioning found in the field of Behaviorism. Once a certain emotional state has become attached to a specific trigger, the brain will fire off the neurochemicals associated with that emotional state every time one experiences the trigger. This is why certain areas we have designated as special to us evoke the same emotional states each time we interact with those areas. If our grandparents' house was a place of love and joy, then years later, even after our grandparents are gone, we can still feel that intense connection with those emotional states when we go to their old home.

Consciously knowing that we can intentionally create a space can give us wonderful feelings of creativity and peace, and we can use that space to become more centered and aligned with our desired emotional state. The following exercise will help you find and enhance a magical space in your home or office which you can use to strengthen positive emotions and access inner resources.

Exercise – Finding Your Magical Space

Step One: Take a moment to become centered. You may want to meditate for a few moments or just quietly sit still. Once you are feeling a sense of calm and focus, allow yourself to quietly walk around your home or office. It may help to keep your eyes closed so that you pay more attention to how you are feeling inside instead of what is around you.

Step Two: When you get to a space where you feel a certain positive emotion you want to experience more often, stop and sit down. Take all the time you need and pay attention to that emotion. If you feel the emotion very strongly, note where you are.

Step Three: Continue moving through the entire area then go back to the area in which you felt the strongest positive emotion. Sit down and allow the emotion flow through you. If you still have a connection to that emotion in that place, you have found your magical space.

Step Four: If possible, claim this space for yourself. Create a place of reverence for it. Some people move the furniture to make it easier to access the space. Others will place objects of importance to them in the space (pictures of ancestors, spiritual images, candles, pictures of nature, etc.). Make a commitment that you will not be in that space unless you want to match the positive emotion you feel it holds. Only do things in that space that align with those positive emotions.

Step Five: Keep your journal handy for when you are in the space to write down any new insights and ideas that come to when you are in the space. Much like the ancient people, you have found a sacred place to enter when you want to change your awareness.

Now that you have your own magical space, you must now decide what you want to create in it. If your space is for creating peace and serenity, then make sure you bring peace and serenity to it. If your space is for creating new goals for your life, then make sure you bring the curious nature for goal setting with you. Any space can become magical if we intend it to be. The family dining room can become a magical place for stimulating conversation and creating deep, emotional connections between family members instead of merely a place to eat. The home office can become a magical place for creation of new financial goals instead of merely a place to file paperwork and pay bills. Decide what you would like to manifest in your magical space. Making the mundane into something magical is within the reach of all of us.

CHAPTER 5: THE FOUR ELEMENTS

We are all in the process of becoming more than we are. Down deep, all of us want to live our lives according to our highest values and ideals. We want our lives to matter and be significant. In spite of having these hopes and dreams, many languish in lives of scarcity and limitation, feeling like the odds are against them or that they don't have what they need to create a life worth living. Even though many people have a quiet yearning to be more than they are, they find ourselves feeling trapped in the lives they currently live. This feeling of being trapped is often due to a stagnant emotional development. The reasons for stagnation are varied but the results of it can be severe. The inability to move forward in any area of one's life can lead to depression, anxiety or a host of physiological problems.

A variety of Western psychological theories and Eastern traditions assert that we as humans are in a process of development. If, at any time in this development, we meet certain challenges which we do not, at that specific time, have the resources to deal with, we may become stuck in a particular stage of our emotional development. Until we work through and transcend that particular stage, we will unconsciously react to the world only through that stage, where we find ourselves stuck. It becomes a circular emotional prison. If we are stuck in this prison, our ability to take action and change our lives will be limited since we can only respond to future challenges with the same responses used in the past. These responses, which may have aided us at the time we first implemented them, often do not work for us today.

Most every ancient culture recognized four elements as the building blocks of the world: earth, water, fire, and air. These elements contained the fundamental essence of everything in the world. In cultures as diverse as China, India, Greece, and Japan the principles of the four elements became fundamental to astrology, diet, healing, agricultural planning, and other aspects of life. The medieval alchemists thoroughly investigated and worked with the four elements in their quest for gold. Many alchemists also understood that these elements did not only correspond to the physical manifestations of each element, but were also metaphoric interpretations for our emotional and spiritual development.

Each one of these elements correlates with where we are in our psychological development. The manifestations of the elements are seen as symbolic representations of the different levels of consciousness available to us. By exploring each one of these elements we can more easily understand what resources we need to move forward in our development and create magical lives. I have found that the model of the four elements seem to connect more with people than the jargon-heavy scientific or psychological terms. The archetypal qualities of the elements make it easier for people to understand at both the conscious and the unconscious levels. This model of psychological development is simple and direct. There are no secret formulas or archaic instructions for working with these elements to make your life better. There are no elaborate ceremonies that need to be completed in order to change how we interact with our world. The things I will ask you to do may appear in many ways to be very ordinary, but often it is in the ordinary where we often overlook the extraordinary and therefore miss magic in action.

The first element, Earth, represents the solid substances found in the world such as rocks. It can also correspond to the raw material of our bodies. On the emotional and psychological level, its positive qualities are stability and strength, and its negative qualities are stubbornness or fear of change.

The second element, Water, represents the various formless and flowing substances of the world. Physical examples are our bodily fluids. On the emotional and psychological level, Water's positive qualities are flexibility and positive emotions such as happiness and curiosity. Its negative qualities are defensiveness and the inability to go with the flow of life.

The third element, Fire, represents energetic, forceful change in the world. Physically, this can take the form of the body's metabolism. On the emotional and psychological level this element's positive qualities include motivation and passion. Its negative qualities include aggression and oppression of others.

The fourth element, Air, represents movement. Physically, this takes the form of breathing. The wind element also refers to the expansion of the mind and the gaining of knowledge. The emotional and psychological dimension of this element consists of positive qualities like compassion, freedom and understanding, and negative qualities are carelessness, selfishness and inconsideration.

According to the ancient sages, these universal elements of Earth, Water, Fire, and Air, make up our human form, and everything that is in our environment. The Greek philosopher Empedocles asserted that the world consisted of four distinct elements which mixed and separated to create material life on earth. It is crucial for our physical, emotional and mental health and wellness to have the correct elemental balance. If the elements are balanced we experience wellness in all areas of our lives and are functional, happy individuals. If, however, there are elemental unbalances, illness and dysfunction can occur. By purifying and working with the energies of each element, one can overcome these issues and experience contentment and peace.

This principle of balance is crucial to our ability in creating a different way of interacting with the world. It is by balancing the positive and negative qualities of each element that allows us to move up the hierarchy of consciousness. If we feel limited at each level, it is usually due to our perceived lack of internal resources. A resource is any emotion, event, belief or behavior we have that can assist us in navigating the challenges life throws at us. For example, if you have developed the inner resource of toughness and determination due to an athletic endeavor, you can use that resource in other areas of your life. If you have developed the resource of compassion by helping people through charity work, then you could also use this resource to assist others in a professional setting.

I believe the reason people do not change and grow is not actually due to limitations. The lack of growth is due to an inability to recognize and use resources we already have. These resources can help facilitate a successful outcome in life. If we recognize that we have the ability to do more than we think we can, that alone can be a resource which can lead to greatness in each person.

At any point we can find ourselves knocked down by life's adversities, such as the loss of a job, relationship, etc. and we lose touch with our inner balance. When we re-balance our thoughts and actions, we re-balance the element which corresponds to the needs we feel are missing. As stated in an earlier magical principle, for every positive in life there is a negative and vice versa.

The emotional and psychological development laid out in the four elements is similar to the work of Western psychologist Abraham Maslow. In 1943, Maslow authored a work entitled "A Theory of Human Motivation," in which he advanced the theory that people have a distinct number of needs, and these needs form a hierarchy. Some of these needs are more basic for survival than others. Maslow's model became known as the "Hierarchy of Needs" and is usually represented as a five level pyramid. Only after the lower, basic needs are met can one move successfully into the higher level needs. Maslow believed that people have an intrinsic desire to move toward their full potential but many become stuck in lower levels of development which limits becoming who they were meant to become.

Maslow labeled the lower four levels as "deficiency needs." This designation was due to the urgency to meet needs such as the physiological needs (food, water, shelter and sleep), safety needs (protection from harm, order, stability and good health), social needs (love, affection and belongingness) and esteem needs (recognition, accomplishment, respect for others and self-worth). Maslow created a fifth level of his pyramid he called "growth needs." This level enables a person to "self-actualize," which means reaching the fullest potential as a human being. Maslow believed that once one has met the deficiency needs, one can then turn his or her focus to self-actualization. These "growth needs" do not come from a necessity but rather from an internal yearning to grow as a person.

As Maslow put it:

"What a man can be, he must be. This need we may call self-actualization...it refers to the desire for self-fulfillment, namely, to the tendency for him to become actualized in what he is potentially. This tendency might be phrased as the desire to become more and more what one is, to become everything that one is capable of becoming."

Maslow's theory is comparable to the concept of the four elements. If we are living our lives stuck in the negative qualities of a specific element, we keep ourselves from growing and evolving into the person we wish to become. Our highest potentials can be realized only when we have gained the resources to transcend the first four elements. This upward movement is not to be accomplished in an accelerated, superficial manner but rather in a methodical partaking of new experiences which can supply us with the resources we need. Once we know that we possess all the resources we need at each of the ascending four elements, we can then enter the realm of inspiration and our highest calling. When we move through each element toward a higher understanding of our place in the world, we unleash an innate drive that moves us to become the best of who we are. We literally feel magically moved to become more of our authentic self.

We cannot reach the higher levels (or elements) if our lower needs are not fulfilled. For example, it is difficult to start a non-profit organization to help abused children if one is preoccupied with finding food and shelter. It is a challenge to be totally present within a personal relationship if attention is focused on struggling with paying bills that appear to have no limit. It is nearly impossible to be an effective business leader if one is fixated on avoiding any form of criticism. All of these lower elements will overtake any aspirations of higher elements. Only by working through our issues at each elemental level can we prepare ourselves for access to our highest level of being. The journey through each element is part of the process of becoming who we really are. We cannot avoid certain elements if we want to gain higher awareness. Much like the stress our muscles experience while lifting weights, in order to become stronger, our mental and emotional development must be challenged in order to grow. By working through our "stuff" we are better equipped to deal with future challenges.

The more often we allow ourselves to obtain all the physical, mental and emotional resources we need to move through each element, the less affected we are by the negative qualities which previously would have immobilized us. By learning effective responses to emotional challenges contained in each element, we move closer to the domain of finding meaning and purpose in our lives. We become more aware of an internal feeling of destiny to truly become the person we dream about, someone who expresses a distinct uniqueness as a human being.

In the following chapters we will closely examine the role each element plays in our interactions and decision making. You will be given exercises for each element to aid in mentally and emotionally balancing the energy at these levels of awareness. Take your time going through each element. This endeavor is not a race, but rather is a delving into our unconscious minds to become open to a potential which we have not recognized in ourselves until now.

CHAPTER 6: EARTH

The first element we will examine is the Earth element. This foundation is crucial to any work we do in the next elements. If we only get as far as balancing our inner thoughts and emotions at the Earth level, this alone can aid in moving us toward happiness and contentment. Without a solid foundation in the Earth realm, we are unable to move upward through the other elements. Every house needs a solid foundation upon which to build, and the Earth is the foundation on which our practice will rest. This is why most of the work will be at this first element.

The Earth element has been viewed by different cultures as having a maternal energy since the earth is the womb from which all material things come. The Earth nurtures us and provides us with shelter and nourishment. This element is also associated with the physical body and the material plane. Earth provides the basis for what one desires in a physical form. It stands for all that is solid. It gives shape and form to all things. It encompasses all of nature including our bodies. In Western esoteric traditions, earth can represent manifestation and creation.

The emotional aspects of the element include stability, endurance and reliability. When we have the Earth element balanced, we feel stable and grounded. We are not so easily knocked off balance by the daily challenges. We feel confident that our needs will be met and that we are capable of taking care of ourselves. We have a feeling of security and safety which enables us to move toward what we want to create in our lives. We feel grounded in our ability to provide for our own needs.

If, however, we do not feel balanced in the Earth element, we may feel as if we are unable to have any stability in life. We are unable to achieve our goals, and we are constantly on the lookout for someone to either save us or worse, to harm us. We feel a resistance to change even though these changes could be beneficial to us. Our fearful overreaction to change could become dysfunctional patterns of behavior such as lashing out at others or isolation. Complacency and apathy are negative qualities associated with the Earth element.

If our way of responding to the world is unconsciously rooted in the negative qualities of the earth element, we can become stuck in fears about survival, scarcity, safety and become consumed with trust issues. These emotions are related to our perception of not having met our basic survival needs. When we feel we do not have the inner resources of stability and safety at key points in our lives, we often become unconsciously stuck at this level. Then we are constantly driven to protect ourselves from physical and emotional harm. Sometimes this unconscious fear creates havoc in our relationships since we are preoccupied with the potential of being hurt by others. In some cases, this unconscious fear of being hurt causes us to lash out toward others in anger, since anger has its basis in fear.

People who do not feel they have access to the positive

qualities of Earth are often consumed with what they feel is missing in life. If the unconscious mind is focused primarily on scarcity and the lack of safety, a person will often feel under attack from the outside world. This person may very well feel that his or her very survival is at risk, even if the situation does not warrant such a reaction. The unconscious mind plays a continuous program which results in feelings of fear and self-preservation. These primitive reactions are due to the autonomic nervous system trained long ago to immediately shift into a fight or flight response whether or not there is a physical threat. Often, it is a person's earlier experiences associated with safety and survival that are unconsciously projected onto the outside world. If our reality is a construction of our unconscious mind, then any event could potentially be experienced as a threat to our survival, even if this is not remotely true.

When we experience this kind of reality, it is not surprising that we frequently feel frightened and out of control. In order to maintain a sense of control and security our thinking may become very rigid with emphasizing exactness in our affairs. This thinking is dichotomous or "black and white." Anything out of the ordinary can cause a negative emotional reaction. An unrelenting, unconscious demand for ensuring to remain static with no change creates anxiety since life in itself is nothing but change.

If these unconscious, earth element needs are not met, the constant fear and long term stress lying beneath the surface can lead to physical illness. I have known many cases of people suffering from what they thought of as a physical

139

ailment, only to find that their symptoms rapidly improved once they had made a breakthrough in their emotional issues. One of my clients, Sandy, came to see me because she was having issues with anxiety. Sandy was constantly nervous and fidgeting. She was a very pleasant person, but she would excessively worry about little things in her life far beyond what was the norm. She believed she could not trust anyone with a task so she took on far too much responsibility, which only created more anxiety and stress for her. As pleasant as Sandy was, it was also obvious how much emotional discomfort she was experiencing.

In addition to her worry, for close to ten years she also had suffered from fibromyalgia, a physical ailment characterized by musculoskeletal pain, excessive fatigue, and issues with memory and sleep. This physical condition kept her from living the lifestyle she enjoyed. She had previously been very active in sporting activities before she began to exhibit the symptoms of fibromyalgia. Making matters worse were the side effects of her medications which caused almost as much discomfort as her illness.

Sandy wanted to get to the root cause of her issue and alleviate her anxiety. We used a process to bypass her conscious mind and explore her unconscious world. We went back to the first time she had recalled feeling anxiety. As she became aware of the memory, she began to intensely cry. She remembered being three years old at the beach and walking with her parents, but somehow became separated from them. She remembered being lost and knocking at the door of a nearby house to ask for help. A disheveled older woman answered the door and brought her inside. Within a few minutes, the older woman insisted that three year old Sandy should start calling her "Mother." The woman, probably suffering from dementia, had decided to keep Sandy believing Sandy was her own daughter.

Sandy was trapped and couldn't get away from this woman who clearly had mental health issues. For several hours Sandy was terrified and was unable to escape from this situation. Later in the evening, there was a knock on the door. Two police officers were going door to door looking for Sandy. As soon as Sandy heard the police officers talking to the older woman she shouted to them and ran out begging for help. The policemen took Sandy to her parents who had spent the past few hours in emotional agony, fearing for the safety of their child.

As Sandy told this story she released all the emotion she had stored at the unconscious level. She was truly terrified as she related the incident from the past. After all her emotion was expended, I suggested that the adult Sandy visualize forgiving the older woman. When Sandy finished our work, she remarked how surprising it was that she had remembered something so far in the past. Over the next two weeks I watched as Sandy's physical health began to rapidly improve. Within one month of her breakthrough session, she was walking most every night for twenty minutes. Within two months she had started going to the gym. She also noticed how she worried less and less about the day to day affairs of living. Her family noticed a major difference in her and expressed their happiness to see the "old Sandy" again.

It appeared that Sandy's anxiety was not only wreaking havoc with her emotions but also with her body. This significant event which had happened more than forty years before was being replayed at the unconscious level every day. Sandy had been constantly worried, and as a result her body continued to release stress hormones which harmed her immune system. Once she was able to let go of her unconscious emotional reaction to this old event, her body began to heal itself. She was able to be physically active and also began to trust in her environment more. Sandy was also able to let go of the little things and stop taking on so much added responsibility.

Erik Erikson, a developmental psychologist, believed that our emotional development occurs in a series of stages. Each stage is marked by a critical period in which we progress or regress in our development. If we are able to positively resolve our emotional crisis at each stage, we can move forward in our development with a healthy sense of self. However, if we cannot resolve a crisis, we may become unconsciously stuck in the stage and act out life patterns based on what is unresolved.

The first stage of Erikson's theory is known as "Trust vs. Mistrust." This is the time period when we are infants. We are totally dependent on our caregivers to nurture us and keep us safe. If we feel safe and protected, we begin to form healthy beliefs about our place in the world. We learn to trust that our caregivers will provide for us and assist us when we are in distress. The positive outcome of this infant stage is the ability to trust that we are able to make our own way in the world with confidence and hope.

The negative outcome of "mistrust" occurs when we are not taken care of by our caregivers. We feel we must constantly be on guard since we never know from where or from whom danger may come. If as infants, our needs are not met, grow up with a fear of establishing connections with others. Based on our early experiences, we cannot risk opening up to another person or unfamiliar situation since we view them as dangerous. We then project our fear of being hurt onto the outside world and frequently find ourselves in situations that reinforce our unconscious belief that we cannot trust others or ourselves.

This is similar to a concept of Sigmund Freud's called the Oral Stage, which also occurs during the first year of life. In this stage, the infant needs to have his or her survival and safety needs met. Freud believed that if we do not obtain the nurturing we need in the very early stage of our lives, as adults we become dependent on others to soothe our anxiety and meet our safety and security needs. If we are unconsciously seeking a parental figure to save us, we enter into relationships looking for someone to emotionally take care of us. We believe that we cannot live without that person since we do not believe we have the capacity to take charge of our own emotional and physical needs. As one person put in a conversation I overheard about a woman's frustration with her fiancé, "He doesn't want a wife, he wants a mother."

On the other hand, if we don't obtain the nurturing and security we need as infants, we may show aggression in order to dominate our environment to ensure that we do not go without what we perceive that we lack. If we do not feel we can obtain our needs through positive interaction, then we will shift to manipulation in order to know that we have security and safety. Someone who shows the aggression side of Freud's theory will be very cynical and paranoid. This person will feel an intense need to protect himself from being hurt.

"Safety is something that happens between your ears, not something you hold in your hands"

-Jeff Cooper

In order to transcend the aspects of the earth element which may hold us back, we need to begin to work toward mastery over these emotional and behavioral parts of ourselves. We need to perform specific actions, think specific thoughts, and allow ourselves to experience new resources which can alleviate our unnecessary mental suffering. When we do all of these together, we experience a profound shift in how we relate to ourselves and our world.

The best place to begin our work is with the body itself. We often do not recognize the emotions we act upon until it is too late. By paying attention to our bodies, we can notice certain feelings as they occur. This will lead to noticing how to move through the feelings without becoming stuck in a repetitive cycle of reactions. By allowing ourselves to feel our emotions, we become aware at the somatic level of what resources we truly need. Ignoring our feelings only represses those emotions further into our unconscious and creates a more ingrained fixation on each element. It is by allowing ourselves to feel that we can move through the negative qualities of each element. We can then balance the negative with positive qualities thus creating health and mobility to higher levels of awareness. The ability to fully feel our emotions, while at the same time being able to examine them, is true spiritual power.

Begin with a memory of a time when you felt angry or frightened. It doesn't matter what the situation was as long as you can strongly bring forth a memory. As the memory forms, notice what your body is feeling. Is there a specific feeling the body is experiencing? Where in the body is this feeling located? What are the qualities of the feeling? Is it a heavy or a light feeling? Is it soft or hard? How intense is that feeling? Allow yourself to completely feel anything that comes as you remember that situation.

As you continue to notice the feelings in your body, let your mind drift to another time when you had a similar feeling. Notice any changes in your body as you allow another memory to come to the surface. Really allow yourself to experience the feelings attached to this second memory. Don't move away from the feelings because they are uncomfortable. Stay with them and examine what happens as you focus on them. Allow any other memories to float up to your conscious mind as you continue to examine how your body feels.

As these memories and feelings make themselves known, avoid judging any actions on your part in the memories. Just notice what the content of the memory is as you feel the feelings connected to the memories. You are in the role of the observer. You are observing your body and your memories, nothing more. Any information which comes to your mind is simply noticed as if it is a billboard on the side of the road which you are driving past.

Just by doing this one exercise you are teaching your body and your mind that you are not your thoughts. You are allowing whatever comes up to only be something that is observed. If you have an emotional reaction to a specific memory, that is fine as long as you allow yourself to observe your body feeling the emotion. The more you permit your feelings to come to your awareness, the more information, which may have been lurking under the surface, will make itself known. This is a good thing since what we push way will always come back, but what we allow to move through us can eventually leave.

I once used this exercise with a woman who was experiencing much grief about her son's deployment in the military. Her son was not in a combat role and more than likely would not see any battle since he worked in computer systems. In spite of this fact, this woman was very fearful and grieved her son's departure. He had been away more than a year with no problems, but she could not seem to stop thinking fearful worried thoughts. She had become consumed with worry and it was ruining her life.

As we began the process of observing emotions, she found that it was very easy to get in touch with her fearful feelings, but she had a hard time allowing herself to observe them. After a little while she found that she could begin to notice the feelings happening in her body without a knee jerk reaction to run away. As we progressed through the exercise, she began having memories of similar events in her life in which she felt a high degree of anxiety. It seemed that most of her life she had been feeling very anxious. We took our time going over each memory and having her notice how her body was feeling.

After some time had passed she suddenly had a memory that came into her conscious mind. She began to feel very upset. I soothingly reminded her to stay with the feeling and just observe it. She did and then began to tell me about the memory that was causing her such discomfort. She was very young and out one evening with her mother to pick up something from one of the downtown stores in her neighborhood. She had been told her father was out of town that evening which happened often due to his work. She and her mother were having a nice time as they strolled down the street.

All of a sudden, they ran into her father who was coming out of the movie theater arm in arm with another woman. The shock she felt, not only from seeing her father with another woman, but from seeing her mother who was usually a positive, happy person become a screaming and aggressive person, was a major event for her. She remembered the arguing between her parents and her mother grabbing her and storming off. She remembered her mother sobbing uncontrollably as they walked home. She had vivid memories of being in bed that night and hearing her mother cry herself to sleep. This was a major painful memory in this woman's life.

As she talked about her memories, I continued to direct her to observe what was happening in her body. She noticed that the tightness of the anxiety was very strong when she accessed this old memory. I asked her to hold on to the feeling she had in her body and allow herself to fully feel it without distracting herself from the emotion. She cried old tears as her body was permitted to fully experience the feelings which had been lying under the surface for many years. After a few minutes she noticed the feeling began to wane. She became aware of the feeling becoming a little lighter. We ended our session when she had fully completed the exercise.

The next time I saw her she told me that she was not nearly as worried about her son being deployed as she had been previously. She believed that her old feelings of losing her idealized image of her father and seeing her mother hurt deeply had made the present situation worse. Since she fully allowed herself to feel the hurt through those old emotional wounds, she had a much more balanced view of her present situation. By allowing ourselves to feel our pain and hurt from the past while we observe our emotions unfold is a way to decrease the reactive charge of past memories and

148

experiences.

Gaining Stability in the Earth Realm

There are several ways in which we can create more stability in our lives. By taking specific actions we can create the conditions in our environment which will gives us the inner resources to balance our energies at the Earth element. This can provide a spring board for our ascent to the other elements. Since the Earth element is primarily associated with stability and security, we need to start a process of creating those conditions in several areas of our lives. Once we feel a sense of strength and balance in these areas, we can relax and focus our attention on other areas of our lives that do not involve reactive fear.

Financial stability

The first area we will address in the earth element is our financial lives. Since being able to take care of ourselves often involves money, we must make our finances a priority. Too often people shy away from dealing with financial issues because it can be uncomfortable to talk about money (and the lack of it). We cannot have mastery over an area of our life which we don't acknowledge. Putting our heads in the sand like an ostrich and hoping for our financial situation to improve all by itself will not give us the inner resources needed to move toward our goals. When we turn away from taking responsibility for our finances, we doom ourselves to dependence upon others who might not always have our best interests at heart. Make a commitment now to start taking charge of your finances.

1. Start saving 10 percent of your income.

We often hear how important it is to pay yourself first. When it comes to creating financial security, it is absolutely the most important thing you can do. If you wait until everyone else has been paid and pay for all your fun activities, you will have little to add to your savings. If you make everyone else in the world a priority over yourself, then you can rest assured that there will be little money left over for financial stability. Begin to value yourself and your future by saving money. The more money you save, the more security you will feel. Imagine if you had a whole year's salary in your bank account. How would that make you feel? If your car had a repair bill would you worry the same way with that much cash in your account? If you had an unexpected visit to the doctor would you worry about the cost as much if you had a year's salary in cash available to you? I'm guessing not.

By putting money away every month, we are actively creating a sense of security in our lives. Even if we put only a few dollars into our savings, we can still feel that we are taking control of our financial destiny. You could set up an automatic draft to take 10 percent out of your checking account and immediately put it into a savings account so that you don't have to struggle to do it. Begin educating yourself on different investment programs through reputable sources. I recommend building up a minimum of six months' salary in a secure savings account before you think about jumping into any investment program. By showing yourself that you can save a substantial amount of money, you send a signal to your unconscious mind that helps to redefine how you respond to money.

2. Focus on spending money only on what is truly important.

Financial security is based on a savings mindset not a spending mindset. Too often people spend money on things that bring them little to no benefit. Get clear on why you are spending money. I am not saying don't purchase things you enjoy, I am merely asking you to pay attention to any knee jerk spending habits you may have. Many people are automatic spenders. Their money flows out long before they realize that it is gone.

I once had a friend who was very generous to others, but he would spend money just because he had money in his pocket. I remember one time when he and I were on a trip and had stopped to get gas at a convenience store. He went in to pay for the gas and came out with a wrestling magazine. I asked him why he bought a wrestling magazine. He replied that he used to watch wrestling when he was a little kid. Even though he had no real interest in wrestling now, he thought it was interesting that there were still wrestling magazines being sold. He never once read the magazine which cost six dollars.

The sad thing was he constantly made purchases like this, and in the process, would spend several hundred dollars a month mindlessly. If he had invested half of the money he mindlessly spent over ten years, he would have quite a nest egg waiting for him.

Avoid being an emotional buyer. If you want something, and it feels like an impulse, wait forty-eight hours and see if you still feel the same way about the purchase. You may find that by taking a little extra time you can often avoid an impulse purchase which you will regret. Advertisers work very hard to convince you of the worth of their product and how scarce it is in the marketplace. Don't be fooled. Just because someone else tells you that you need a product, it is not gospel.

3. Avoid going into any additional consumer debt

Consumer debt keeps many people from a true sense of security. If you are in massive debt due to credit card spending, then you have a serious problem which needs to be dealt with immediately. Don't think of it as anything but a problem. If your automatic reaction is to spend money that you don't have to purchase something you want immediately, then you have a serious problem. The good news is that if you recognize it as a problem, you can begin to solve it. Begin putting your energy into paying down your consumer debt as quickly as possible. It is difficult to live a magical life of freedom if you are beholding to others. Declare yourself to be free of all debts (financial and emotional).

Physical stability

When we know that our physical safety is not in jeopardy we can begin to relax in many areas of our lives. If we constantly worry about being hurt or not being able to take care of ourselves, we cannot focus on our other goals. If our basic needs for physical security are not met it matters little to us if we get a promotion at work or if someone values our friendship. Once we have a sense of power and control over our physical well-being we can begin moving that stability to other areas of our lives.

1. Learn to defend yourself

By learning to physically defend ourselves in a dangerous confrontation we can unleash a feeling of confidence and certainty that words cannot adequately describe. We cease feeling fearful in our interactions with others and become more open and comfortable in our own skin. By knowing that we can protect ourselves we send out a vibe of self-assuredness that will be noted immediately by others. This is not the same as being cocky or a loud mouth tough guy but rather being someone who finds it easy to look other people in the eyes and clearly state what he or she wants out of life.

I recommend seeking instruction on how to defend yourself from real experts. There is both a physical and mental component in dealing with violence, and a good self-protection program will cover both. If you want to take a martial art class, I advocate making sure that you can test the skills you learn against an opponent who resists and fights back in a safe environment. Today many martial arts schools use safety equipment that allows their students to go all out in training but without sustaining injuries.

Let me be clear here. I do not advocate violence against other people. I only endorse the positive effects of knowing you can defend yourself against an aggressive opponent who attempts to harm you and/or your loved ones. True stability in the Earth element is not about seeking fights or starting confrontation. It is about maintaining your personal boundaries and being able to protect yourself from harm. A funny thing happens when you know that you can defend yourself; you start to let go of the automatic fear reaction of being a victim. You begin living your life from a place of strength rather than constantly focusing on how you could be hurt.

I studied martial arts for many years but deep down I didn't feel that I could really defend myself. One day I began training in a system that tested the skills being taught against a resisting opponent immediately after learning them. This was so that I could be sure that I could do what I had learned in class in "real time." I felt a tremendous shift in how I felt about myself. I noticed I no longer worried about having to confront others or interacting with aggressive people. I found a quiet place inside myself where I knew I could be safe. Even though I did not seek fights and avoided any potentially violent situation, I knew that I could take care of myself. That inner knowledge gave me the confidence that I could do more things than I thought I could. My ability to protect myself gave me the confidence to try new things and interact with new people. Fear began to evaporate leaving calm and peace in its place.

2. Learn outdoor survival

If we are terrified of losing everything we own and becoming homeless, many of our decisions about our future can be limited. Even though we rationally we don't think we would end up on the streets, a part of us may fear that could happen. This fear of going without food and shelter brings up one of our biggest fears: death. When we feel we may die due to a lack of food and shelter, a part of us is paralyzed from moving forward toward our goals. When we are unconsciously fearful that at any minute we may be without the items we need to survive, it seems that nothing else matters. A great way to overcome this debilitating fear is to learn to survive with nothing but our bodies.

When we learn to survive in the wilderness we discover that all we really need to live is our creativity. If we are not dependent on others or on having an income, we begin to see the world differently. We figure out that we don't have to have a job in order to survive. We see that we can meet our basic needs for food, water and shelter even if the worst happens. It is not luxury living, but it certainly is not dying.

Find a good survival program near you which takes several days to a week to teach you the basics of outdoor survival. Try to get into a program that keeps you outdoors the whole time to ensure that you do have the skills to make it. Once you see that you can take care of yourself in harsh conditions, you may find that your fear about the unknown begins to decrease over time.

I once worked with a client who had issues with feelings of abandonment by significant people in her life. When she was a child, she was abandoned by her parents and raised by a relative who was fairly insensitive to her needs. As she grew up, she began to have severe episodes of worry about people in her life. She feared that romantic partners would leave her. This caused a great strain on her relationships and, ultimately, it resulted in the very thing she wanted to avoid. Her partners left her. She detested how needy she appeared to be, but yet she felt that if she were alone something terrible would happen to her. She did not believe she could make it on her own.

I sent her out to find a company to teach her wilderness survival skills so that she could survive even if she were totally all alone. She enjoyed camping so she was up for the challenge. In the span of one week she learned how to eat off the land, find and purify water, and build a shelter which would keep her warm in below freezing temperatures. She even spent several nights sleeping in her shelter to find out if she would be comfortable, which she was. When she returned to her therapy session she felt more in control of her own life knowing she could fend for herself in the most primitive of situations. In time her abandonment fear decreased so that she was able to connect with a partner without appearing needy or fearful.

Emotional stability

1. Allow yourself to trust more

Trusting is difficult for many people. If we have a history of being disappointed in others whom we thought we could trust, it can seem almost dangerous to let our guard down. As you may recall from the work of Erik Erikson, trust is the primary emotional stage of our early childhood on which all the other stages are often built. Once we begin to trust more, a whole world begins to open up for us.

Start by choosing one person whom you feel is worthy of trusting. Tell them something personal about yourself with the premise that he or she is not allowed to share this information with anyone else. This secret does not need to be something monumental. It may be just about how you feel in the moment, if that is something you rarely share with others. It could be a favorite positive memory of yours. It could be a fun fact that no one else knows about you. Whatever the secret is, just take the risk to throw it out to him or her. You will never gain trust by hiding from others. It is only in sharing and interaction that we can trust.

Notice how it feels to share with another. Gage how the process of sharing went. If, after a few days or weeks, the person you shared with has kept your confidence, share a little more information. If, on the other hand, this person has not kept your confidence then realize that this is only one person's actions and not everyone else in the world. Find a new person to begin the process of trust building. The more people you can start confiding in, the more you will see that there are other people with whom you can relax around and can trust. Make sure you keep their confidence as well when they share with you.

2 Get massages as often as possible

Even though this may sound "touchy feely," the truth is that people love and need to be touched. In fact, it may be crucial to our ability to grow. A study conducted at Duke University found that the holding and caressing of a newborn infant can actually activate certain genes which contributes to physical growth. These researchers found out that a target gene known as Orinthine Decarboxylase is expressed due to the presence of maternal touch. The researchers also found that if this touch does not occur there is a marked reduction in the ability of our cells to multiply, and there can be a suppression of the cells' responses to the presence of growth hormones. This also results in abnormal patterns of neuro-endocrinal secretion which directs and regulates things like our metabolism, behavior, and blood pressure. Essentially, we needed to be touched and cared for in order for our bodies and minds to fully develop to their full potential.

If we have missed out on that part of our development we can always begin the process of being touched on a regular basis. Touch does not have to be a sexual activity. Therapeutic massage is a great way to not only work out muscle soreness, energy blocks and tension in our bodies, it is also a fantastic way to relax and increase an overall sense of wellness. I recommend getting at least one massage a week from a trained and ethical practitioner. Find a massage therapist who has experience working with a variety of people. Ask for recommendations for a good massage practitioner from other people.

Getting regular massages will not only help your nervous system relax, but it will also aid your mind in learning to let go and trust another person. It can help us release control when we allow a professional to work our sore muscles and stretch our limbs in order to give us back some of our original suppleness and flexibility. You may be surprised how quickly you notice a difference in how you feel in your body with regular massage therapy.

3. Start challenging your thoughts

An important part of obtaining stability at the Earth level is to become more aware of the thoughts we are thinking. As we discussed in the previous chapter, our thinking has a tremendous impact on how we view ourselves and the world around us. In order to gain more peace in our lives, we need to be in charge of the thoughts we think. Just because we think a thought does not make it true nor does it make it helpful.

Begin taking some time every day to notice what thoughts naturally come to your consciousness, Begin to spot if there are recurring themes to your thoughts. Pay attention to when certain thoughts arise. See if you can spot a relationship between certain thoughts and certain feelings. Examine which thoughts create a feeling of happiness and which thoughts create anxiety or frustration. If you do nothing more than this, you will find some surprising information about how your mind has been working. Until now these thoughts have been automatic and habitual.

After you have spent some time noticing your thoughts, begin the process of challenging the thoughts which cause you to feel less than resourceful. A good way to do this is the use of the ABC model developed by psychologist Albert Ellis. Ellis, the creator of Rational Emotive Behavior Therapy, found that people were often psychologically immobilized often not by things which happen to them but rather by their thoughts about what has happened to them. He asserted that the beliefs we carry with us determine our levels of happiness. If we accept flawed thoughts without question, we may be causing ourselves undue misery.

Ellis' ABC model is very simple but very effective in discovering if our thoughts are irrational or distorted. 'A' stands for the activating event. This is the event that occurs to us. 'B' is our belief about 'A'. This is our belief about the event which has occurred. Lastly, 'C' is the consequence of our belief. This consequence could be an emotion or an action. The formula is simply $A+B = C$. What we think about what happens to us determines how we act and feel after the event.

Here is an example: You turn in a project at work of which you were proud to your boss. The boss tells you that he is not happy with your work and requests you to do it over. You feel depressed and in a state of despair.

A (activating event) – The boss did not like your work

B (belief about the activating event) – You believe you are incompetent or a failure

C (consequence which happens as a result of your belief) - depression

Most people believe $A = C$ and this belief justifies their reactions and limitations. This is not true. If we honestly examine our thoughts, we will see that in order to feel a certain emotion, there has to be a thought behind it. If we have limited beliefs, then we will have limited access to positive emotional states. To gain stability in our emotions, we must consciously adjust our beliefs from thoughts of limitation and dysfunction to beliefs of possibility and reason. This is how the previous example would be different if we changed the 'B' part of this formula:

A (activating event) – The boss did not like your work

B (belief about the activating event) – You don't agree but realize everyone has different opinions

C (consequence which happens as a result of your belief) – mild annoyance but acceptance of the situation

By being aware of our thoughts we can transform the quality of how we interact with our world. We will no longer feel that we are victims of our environment but will see ourselves as co-creators of our daily interactions. Life will certainly hand us dilemmas, but it is the quality of our thinking that will determine how we deal with those complications. When we challenge our thoughts, we can increase our ability to feel emotional stability. When we feel we are in charge of ourselves, the rest of the world will be a much easier animal to tame.

Visualization and Meditation for Accessing the Earth Element in the Unconscious Mind

Now we turn our attention to the realm of the unseen mind. The previous directives were to train our conscious minds to access the resources we need to begin our transformation at the Earth level. This section is dedicated to opening up to the unlimited resources which are available to us at the unconscious level. By working with both our conscious and unconscious mind, we supply ourselves with a

162

complete integration which can yield great results and insights.

The following visualization and meditation is designed to connect you with the earth element at the unconscious level by using archetypal images. Even though consciously you may not understand the significance of what you will read, at the unconscious level your mind will connect with the qualities of the earth element which you may be either missing or qualities to which you may need to be reintroduced. I recommend reading this part of the book into a recording device and playing it as you meditate on its subject matter. If you don't meditate, I recommend reading it out loud to yourself every day first thing in the morning and the last thing before bed.

Find a place in your home where you cannot be disturbed for a little while. It doesn't matter where you sit as long as you keep your back straight and are comfortable. Take five slow and long inhale and exhales of breath. Relax your jaw. Feel free to close your eyes.

Imagine yourself walking in a beautiful wooded area. This is a safe, quiet area that gives you so much comfort. You can relax as you walk in this very special place. You can walk as slowly as you like in this safe wooded area. As you are walking you notice that the trees are a vibrant green. You notice how firm the ground feels under your feet. The trail you are walking on gives you an excellent view of the forest around you. You can hear the sounds of different birds in the trees calling out in quiet but beautiful songs. You may notice the sound of a waterfall in the distance with its comforting roar. The temperature on your skin is very comfortable and pleasing. The weather is just the right temperature to truly enjoy this peaceful scene.

You decide to continue your walk in a direction which you have never previously explored. You slowly take your time noticing a variety of different sights, including bright green ferns growing from the ground in a pattern which looks like they had been specifically planted for your enjoyment. The dark brown bark of the trees seems very vivid as you take in this new space. There is a small pond which has formed in the ground which reflects the small bit of sunlight which peeks occasionally through the trees. This new path you have taken is presenting you with many magical sights of nature to behold. You feel a sense of peace as you effortlessly move through this area.

As you are walking along this path, you come across an extremely large stone. As you walk around the side of the stone you see that it is the opening to a cave. You pat the stone with your hand feeling how hard and solid this large stone feels. You think to yourself how long this rock has been here. This cave may have even been formed from the beginning of time. You see green moss covering the top of the entrance of the cave. You marvel at how nature continues to remain after so many years. The entrance to the cave feels inviting and familiar. It is as if you have been to this place many times but yet it seems to be a new experience for you. There is a feeling of comfort as you begin to move inside the cave.

Even though you are going down deeply into the earth, it feels warm and relaxing. You feel such peace as you begin to explore this ancient place. You again pat your hand on the walls of the cave and hear the solid sound of the rock. It gives you a sense of security knowing how firm the walls of the cave are. You notice a pleasant smell that moves through the cave. You move deeper and deeper into this mysterious yet peaceful place. The temperature is surprisingly warm and the light slightly darkens but only in a way that allows you to relax as you continue to explore.

You hear the sounds of your footsteps on the firm ground in the cave. The shuffle of your walking and the firmness of the ground give you an experience of how it must have felt to prehistoric people who investigated this remarkable place. The lighting continues to dim but your eyes adjust to the difference in light as you find you enjoy the changes in your sensory experiences. You stop and hear a sound of water moving in a slow stream. You are not able to tell if it is ahead of you in the cave or if it is the waterfall far behind you. The sound gives a pleasant feeling to your ears.

You finally come to a place which looks like it has been cleared away by someone from many years ago. As sit down on the ground you begin to feel a strong feeling of being here at some other time in your life. It feels very familiar but yet brand new. You lean back against the cave wall and feel it support your back. You quietly sit and take in any sounds around you. The lighting is very dim but yet you can see the walls of the cave which look to have been carved into and painted long ago by a group of people that time has forgotten.

The images drawn are of people and animals living together in a natural way. The images are wonderful to behold. You notice how relaxed your stomach and hips are as you continue resting against the wall of the cave.

You think to yourself how great it feels to be in this safe and secret place. A part of you truly doesn't want to leave as you feel so much contentment. Another part of you relishes the idea that you could come back to the place any time you want. At any time you desire to relax undisturbed you can always come back to the cave and allow yourself to experience this ancient, strong structure. You feel a smile cross your face as you drift off into a nice sleep knowing you are very safe and secure deep in this hidden protected place. The warmth of the cave envelopes you in a blanket of comfort as you allow yourself to continue drifting into a peaceful slumber.

As you sleep deeply, you begin to dream. You dream of yourself walking through the woods but you are not a human but rather a large bear. As you walk through this forest you feel a deep sense of comfort as you know you are the largest animal in the forest. Your strong arms and legs propel you through the foliage which you enter with no fear as nothing can harm you. As your paws plant firmly on the ground you hear you own voice in your mind tell you that you are the protector of the forest. This thought is pleasing to you as you know how powerful you really are compared to the other animals. Even though you are being a protector you also know how important it is to allow nature to unfold in its own way.

As you come out of the underbrush you see a sparkling creek before you. You cross this creek easily as your large paws enable you to get a solid footing in the stream. After crossing the creek you see a shaded place to rest. You go and sit down leaning your large furry back against an old tree. As you are sitting comfortably you notice a small bear cub come up to you. The cub crawls into your lap. You put your paws tightly around the cub and let it know that you will protect it no matter what happens. The cub is very comfortable and quiet as it nestles down into your strong, powerful arms. You both go to sleep as you sink back into the large tree at your back.

You wake up from your dream about being a bear feeling refreshed. The stone cave wall against your back has supported you as you slept. You look down into your hands to find two rocks that are warm to the touch. You wonder how they got there but a part of you knows there is more to the story than what meets the eye. You put the small rocks in your pocket and begin your ascent out of the cave. As you come to the mouth of the cave you find a large set of bear prints which were not present when you went in the cave. You see that these fresh bear tracks go into the cave from where you just have come. You touch the hard rocks in your pocket and begin to wonder.

CHAPTER 7: WATER

The next element in our progression is Water. The element of water is necessary for life. We need water since it makes up the bulk of our bodies, and many scientists believe we evolved out of the oceans over the course of millions of years. Our connection to water can be seen through our enjoyment of the beach, and lakes. Watching soothing streams and creeks is soothing to us. Many people dream of having a home near a body of water. Water's properties cause a different experience in our minds and bodies. Many sacred temples were positioned near water because the ancients knew that the properties of water activate something deep within our unconscious minds.

Historically, water has been seen as a cleansing and healing element. Many cultures utilize water in rituals in which the old part of a person is washed away, giving rise to a new person who interacts with the world in a much different way. Purification rites for various traditions usually involve water in some manner. The Japanese Yamabushi, who are hermit monks who follow a pantheistic blend of Buddhism, Taoism and Shinto teachings, often stand under cold waterfalls while chanting in order to cleanse their bodies and minds so they can reach higher realms of awareness. Baptism in Christian churches involves some form of water to cleanse the old person into a new person who has accepted Christ as his or her savior. Many of the churches of the recent past met on the banks of the local lake. The preacher entered the water and invited anyone who wished to be "saved" to enter the water and begin a new spiritual life.

One can look through ancient mythology and find many stories which involve water. Since all life originated out of water, it is not unusual to find fountains, springs and wells which are considered sacred spiritual places. They represent the mysterious flow of spiritual power which comes from deep inside the earth into our everyday reality. According to the great mythologist, Joseph Campbell, water often represents consciousness in ancient myths. Many depth psychologists view water as an element of the unconscious and of the timeless mysteries of the soul. Many stories in the Bible have elements of water, which may represent an important change in consciousness for one of the characters. An example would be how often spiritual insight is gained in conversations at a well where one of the participants is drawing water. In other ancient stories, water has also been associated with paranormal abilities and magical rituals.

There is a spring about an hour away from my home where people have been obtaining water for centuries. Many people swear that the spring water has healing properties and can cure many ailments. The land which holds the spring was literally deeded to God by the previous owner, so that everyone could freely obtain the water for aid in their healing. I visited the site one day to see what all the excitement was about, and I found many people filling large containers of the spring water. Several of these people told me that the water can heal almost any disease. One man told me that he once had a small tumor which the doctors wanted to remove.

169

However, he stated he started drinking a half gallon of the spring water every day for a month. He smiled as he told me that when he went back to his doctor, he was shocked to see that the tumor had shrunk in size. The doctor even wondered if he should remove it all. The man and his wife swore by the spring water believing it to be magical and having mysterious healing qualities. They both still drink it every day. One woman I met at the spring confessed that she didn't really know much about the healing properties, but she liked the water because it tasted good in her coffee. I decided to bring home a jug of the water, and I do agree that it tastes good in one's coffee.

In many esoteric traditions, perception, imagination, and self-discovery are connected with water. Water represents the emotions and passions that rule us, and it is this element which metaphorically forms the basis of our personalities and influences our relationships. In Western mystery traditions, water frequently represents the direction of West and the season of autumn.

In order to balance the energies of this element within us, we must make an effort to thoroughly investigate our emotions and the role they play in our lives. Expanding our awareness about ourselves is impossible if we do not honestly look into our own emotions. When we positively access this element, we become more comfortable with expressing ourselves and experiencing the emotions of others. Negative qualities of the water element are our rash action with little to no thought and an inability to control our emotions. Being unable to access our emotions at all can also be a sign of negative aspects of the water element.

Emotions are what give us joy and pain in life. How we respond to what happens to us usually determines the quality of our lives. Our responses are based upon emotions. If our emotions are not congruent with what we want to create in our lives, we will find endless roadblocks and frustrations in the way. By being able to access and use our emotions in a responsible manner, we gain enormous mental power to deal with the inevitable challenges life throws at us.

If we have too much of the water element in our personalities, we can become emotionally erratic. We may sling our emotions all over the people who are close to us. We don't know how to turn off our feelings, and we expect everyone to accommodate us. We can be happy one second and then easily irritated the next. We can feel on top of the world with joy for a little while and then allow something small to take us down to despair. Water represents a flow, but if the flow of our emotions is too erratic, it resembles a rocky whitewater rafting expedition in which everyone is tossed around by the severe current. The flow is so unpredictable that everyone in the raft is in fear and clings to the raft in the hopes of surviving.

This is reminiscent of Freud's concept of the "anal-expulsive" personality. Someone with this type of personality has little control over their emotions. This person will have trouble adhering to any type of structure and will often create disorganization and chaos as an unconscious attempt to control his or her environment. Any attempt to control

171

emotion is perceived as a submission to authority, and this person needs to constantly defy even when it is not beneficial.

I once knew a woman named Marie who rode the waves of her emotions while also feeling she was totally helpless to control them. She was happy when things went her way, but she became furious and emotionally abusive when things did not go her way. She snapped at people at the drop of a hat and then appeared genuinely shocked when they became angry. She believed that she had the right to freely express her emotions, but she rarely allowed anyone else the same option. When someone became upset with her due to her acidic emotional responses, she often despaired, wondering what kind of horrible person she was to have treated someone the way she did. All of these erratic emotional expressions kept Marie from taking responsibility for how she felt. When she was in the midst of her intense emotions she thought she could not reign in her expression of those emotions. As a result whoever was with her was held as an "emotional hostage" to her moods. It became clear that until she was able to get help for the dysregulation in her moods, it would be difficult for her to have satisfying relationships.

On the flip side, if we have too much positive quality in the water element, our emotions are extremely calm, way too calm. We do not feel much excitement or passion in our lives as our flow of emotion is like a very slow creek which creeps by at a snail's pace. We are the epitome of boredom and are emotionally sedentary. There is little to no fun in our lives as we approach everything through logic and reason. We overly calculate before we make decisions. If the water element is too positive, we appear as if we are human computers who do not experience life, but rather analyze it. There is little to no spark in a person's life who is detached from their emotions.

This is similar to Freud's concept of the "anal-retentive" personality. This person becomes emotionally stuck in an unconscious attempt to control every part of life with little tolerance of ambiguity. This person will often appear extremely orderly and rigid with little emotion, because emotions feel dangerous and may upset the order and structure the person craves.

I once worked with Henry and his wife in marital therapy. He was stuck with no access to his emotions. He used logic and reason to guide him. This was a good thing except in the area of emotional connections. His wife found herself feeling alone since Henry lived in his head and not in his heart. He loved his wife, but he didn't know how to access that part of him which allowed emotions to flow freely. A part of him was concerned that if he began to feel emotions, he might lose control which was frightening to him. His wife joked that she had married "Mr. Spock," the character from the television show Star Trek, a Vulcan, who did not feel nor express emotions. Henry's stoic nature led his wife to believe that he did not care for her, which was far from the truth. With time, effort, and therapy, Henry was able to begin tapping into some of his emotions. He would never be the life of the party or an intensely emotional person, but the little bit of emotion that he allowed himself to feel was a welcome change for his wife. This created more closeness in their marriage.

In order to balance these energies we need to actively examine how we are feeling and what we are doing as we go through the day. When things go our way, we need to examine how we are responding. Are we allowing ourselves to feel joy and surprise, or are we keeping ourselves from fully allowing those emotions to emerge? If something doesn't go our way, do we lose our responsibility for our emotions and spew anger at the world? Are we allowing ourselves to feel disappointment and then to create solutions for the situation?

The following exercise has been created to help you learn to balance those energies which rule the water element. Take as much time each day as you need to perform this exercise. The more effort you put in it, the more you will get out of it.

Exercise – Balancing Emotions

1. Find a place where you will not be disturbed for at least fifteen to twenty minutes. Sit in position in which you are comfortable but can remain alert. Begin slowing your breathing down by taking slow inhales and slow exhales of air. Do this for a minute or two in order to become more relaxed. This will help in performing the exercise.

2. Once you are sufficiently relaxed, allow your mind to drift back to a time you felt very happy. Notice what images come to your mind. Really allow yourself to focus on those images and situations from your past. Begin paying attention to how your body feels as you access those memories of happiness from your past. Really allow those feelings to intensify for a moment or two. After you have fully experienced those feelings of happiness, let those memories and feelings fade away on your command.

3. Now clear your mind for a minute or so. Begin to allow your mind to drift back to a time when you were very angry. Really allow yourself to focus on whatever images and situations from your past come up. Pay attention to how your body feels as you access those memories of anger from your past. Intensify those feelings for a moment or two. After you have fully felt those feelings of anger, let those memories and feelings fade away on your command.

4. Again, clear your mind. Now bring up a time when you were really curious about something. Allow yourself to drift back in time to feel that curiosity fully in your body. Notice how the sensation of curiosity feels as you allow it to freely travel all over. Notice whatever images and situations come to mind which allow you to become even more curious. Intensify those feelings of curiosity for several moments. On your command, let those sensations and images fade away.

175

5. Now clear your mind. Go back to the situation or images which caused you to feel anger. As you allow your anger to rise, begin to allow the sensation of curiosity to arise. Continue to focus on the thing which caused your anger but apply the sensation of curiosity to it. Notice what is different in how you perceive the situation now. Pay attention to how your body feels when you become curious about your anger. When you have fully experienced this shift in your emotion, decide to allow those memories to fade away.

6. Finally return to the first image and memory which caused you to feel happiness. Freely allow the feelings of happiness to flow through your body until you are ready to end the exercise.

This exercise is a form of emotional alchemy, in that we are mixing our emotions in an effort to balance them more effectively. By deciding what emotion to bring up and when to end it, we are now showing our unconscious mind that we do have the resources available to control how we feel as we can start and stop them on our command. We are also paying attention to how emotions feel in our bodies. This will aid not only in controlling them but also in experiencing them if we rarely allow ourselves to do so.

Do this exercise for every day for four weeks. Write down in your journal what you noticed after every session. Keep track of how you are feeling and acting about situations in your daily life and notice small changes along the way.

Since a quality of the element of water is flow, we also need to investigate where in our lives we are not allowing a flow to occur. Often life changes cause us to react in ways in which keep the natural flow of life from happening. Changes in job, relationships, finances and other areas are a part of life, but when we become so attached to the outcome we envision for ourselves, we can cause more suffering by holding on and attempting to stop the flow of nature.

When things change, and we are not ready for the change, we will cling for dear life to the old way to which we are accustomed. This not only is ineffective, but it also causes us much mental anguish. In order to go with the flow, we have to courageously accept that the universe may have a direction it is going that is different from where we think we should be going. If we can let go and flow with the natural ebb and flow of nature, we may find that new possibilities far beyond what we ever envisioned for ourselves springing forth.

When water comes to a barrier, it naturally flows around the barrier to find another direction. We often take the opposite approach in that when we hit a barrier, we continue to bang against it over and over until we destroy ourselves rather than adjust our course. We mistakenly believe we know better than nature so we keep smashing against the barrier until there is not much left of us. After that we then blame everyone and everything, rather than adjust our course and become open to new possibilities.

Changing course does not mean giving up. It simply means that the method you are using to achieve a specific outcome is not working. By allowing some degree of flexibility in our approach, we may find that obtaining our goals becomes much easier and more fun than we previously had thought. The more flexible we can be to adapt to what comes, the more we can avoid unnecessary hassle. By going with the flow, we find ourselves drifting "merrily, merrily down the stream" instead of forcing and pushing upstream with excessive pain and effort.

Exercise – Going with the Flow

1. Write down a situation you are presently going through which is giving you a hard time emotionally.

2. List all the ways you have tried to "solve" the problem that have not worked.

3. After you have written all the ways you have tried to solve the problem, write down the barrier in the problem that you keep bumping against.

4. Now write down one specific action that you have repeatedly taken (but hasn't worked) that you could let go in dealing with this problem.

5. Write down how you would feel if you decided to let go of that one action.

6. Repeat with all other actions you have taken until you can feel that you are not bumping against the barrier anymore.

7. Notice how you feel when you think of letting go of the need to control the problem.

Thinking about life as a natural flow is in line with our connection to nature. There is a time in which the plants grow, and there is a time for plants to go dormant. Our lives are like this as well. If we remember that life is an alchemical process, we can understand that the flow of life is a cycle of creation and destruction which will lead to more creation and destruction. By accepting this natural flow we can ride the wave of life without becoming washed away by our inflexibility to adapt to changes. I have found that the person with the most flexibility in any endeavor usually performs the best and navigates challenges more effectively.

Take some time away from your regular routine to travel to a place which has a stream flowing. Sit quietly and watch the flow of the water and the debris which glides along with it. Notice how little resistance is involved in this natural unfolding process. Think to yourself how you can adjust your life to become more like this stream. Life becomes much more magical when we allow the forces of nature to guide us instead of forcing our own will on the natural world.

Water meditation/visualization

The following visualization and meditation is designed to help connect you with the Water element at the unconscious level. As previously noted, I recommend reading this part of the book into a recording device and playing it as you meditate on its subject matter. Go to a place where you will not be disturbed and sit comfortably with your back straight. Take five very slow, long inhales and exhales of breath. Relax your jaw and become centered.

Imagine yourself walking through a beautiful forest. The day is warm but very comfortable. You are enjoying the cool breeze which flows across your skin as you move slowly and effortlessly through the forest. You notice how green the foliage is becoming which lets you know you are nearing a place where water is flowing. Each step you take, you begin to find yourself easily and comfortably moving across the ground. You continue walking as you begin to hear the faint sounds of water trickling in the distance. The closer you walk in the direction of the sound, the greener the foliage becomes. As you slowly go further down a corner of the forest, you see a large creek in front of you. This creek is very wide and fairly deep, but yet you see can the bottom of the creek easily as the water is so very clear. You have never seen water as clear as it is in this creek. You notice that the water moves very smoothly and has a slow but steady current. You marvel at how beautiful this place is and how much everything depends on this water source for life.

You turn to find a canoe behind you that beckons you to use it in the creek. You decide to explore this gorgeous area by way of the creek with the use of the canoe. You easily and gently slide the canoe into the slow flowing creek water and then step inside the canoe. After you have done this, you realize there is no oar for you to use to guide the canoe. You laugh as you have no choice but to allow the slow current to take you as you explore using the canoe. Slowly you move through the water. The canoe effortlessly glides along with the natural flow of water.

As you continue to comfortably glide down the creek, you see that there is a large rock in the middle of the creek. You wonder if you will bump against the rock. As soon as you think this thought you find that the current naturally flows around the rock taking you with it. It appears to have just happened all by itself with no effort on your part. You notice the pretty plants and trees which line the banks of this creek as you glide by easily. All of these elements seem to appear exactly as they need to be without the interference of humans. These elements of nature know just when it is time to grow and where to position themselves.

Moving slowly though the water you allow yourself to relax even more as the canoe continues to flow around any potential barriers that appear to be in its way. You wonder how the water always finds the easiest way to flow and does just what it is supposed to do without any effort on anyone else's part. A sense of peace falls over you as you gently flow along with the water to new places to see and experience on this journey of discovery. It feels to you as if this journey has been waiting to be had by you for many years. The flow of

181

your thoughts slows down, much like the water, to give you a sense of peace and calm to enjoy.

You now come to a large log hanging down from above that is blocking the path of the creek. The water flows around and over the log but there is not enough room for your canoe to get through this barrier. In order to get pass this barrier you struggle to move it by force. You push with all your might but it does not move at all. The more you push, the more the log appears to become wedged in and block the creek. Suddenly you have an insight. You notice that the water flows around the log. You think to yourself and ponder how you can also flow around the log and then you come up with an idea. You lie down in the canoe so no part of you can be seen and allow the water to take the canoe where it supposed to go. Within a moment the canoe has somehow found a way to easily go around this log. It gently and easily moved around the barrier in a way that you would have never thought of in your previous efforts to move the log. You laugh at your folly of trying to force the log out of the way and continue on your wonderfully relaxing trip down the creek.

As you look around you realize that you somehow have arrived back at the place where you started. You pull the canoe to the bank of the creek knowing that you will return again and again to experience this wonderfully relaxing place. Now that you know you can easily and naturally flow along with the creek, you find a comfortable feeling inside yourself that lets you know that your future journeys can be just as peaceful as the moment you just had. You continue your walk into the forest and enjoy the warm comfortable weather and the sounds of the water in the background.

Chapter 8: Fire

The third element we explore is the element of fire. Physically and metaphorically this element can be both destructive and creative. A fire can destroy a forest very quickly, yet the after effects of the burning offer the forest nutrients to grow new and healthier foliage. Fire can be a life saver if one is stranded in the wilderness, but it can also be a life taker if one's property catches fire and burns without boundaries. Fire is an element that causes apprehension and fascination. We are somehow compelled to focus on a campfire at night. With an unbroken stare, we feel its heat. The flames of the campfire can be hypnotic and enchanting we are unconsciously transported back in time to a period of human evolution when nighttime fires were necessary for survival.

The element of fire is also in our model of magical living as the transformer which changes objects and situations with intensity. The fire element has traditionally been associated with passion, motivation and the power of the will. Leadership is a quality associated with fire. Fire represents the will of an individual to create an outcome. It has been seen as the main creative force in each person's soul, which motivated Plato to believe that the element of fire comes the closest to divine reality. Fire represents the direction of South and the season of summer.

The positive qualities of this element are our ability to take action and achieve outcomes which align with our priorities in life. Our skill at exerting control over important situations gives us a sense of power. This power provides us with the capability to create amazing consequences in our endeavors. By harnessing the fire element, we are able to direct our lives with precision and effectiveness. We are able to move closer to having and doing the things we want. We approach challenges with a fixed determination to overcome all the obstacles which may lie in our path. Our inner drive and will power are utilized in effective ways to create magical results for ourselves.

The archetype of the positive quality of fire is found in extremely successful business people, the super achievers who seem to have obtained everything due to their own hard work and determination. The self-help industry is full of examples of the "rags to riches stories" which demonstrate that, with hard work, determination and laser sharp focus, people can achieve amazing things. However, too much emphasis on the positive quality of fire can result in an individual who never seems to stop achieving. There is a feeling of emptiness when they are not pushing toward another goal. The consistent running in the "rat race" will appear in those who have placed too much importance on the positive element of fire.

The negative qualities of the fire element include being held back in reaching our goals because of a lack of confidence in our ability to succeed. Some people who have more negative qualities in this element often have a preoccupation with exercising control over others. They will feel helpless in controlling their own lives, and as a result, may have trouble yielding power to others. These type of people either aggressively imposing power over others or, the opposite, in embracing submission and meekness. They may lack the ability to view others as equals, instead viewing them as either superiors or secondary. This results in constant fears of being inadequate, overwhelmed by the competition, and having an overall loss of power.

Over my year of living magically, I realized that in the past I had been too focused on the positive qualities of fire within myself. I have always been a fairly driven person, but I found that my life had become one long goal check off list. It always seemed that I needed some new goal to chase in order for me to feel good about myself. I believe that we all need goals in life, but I found that a constant state of pushing toward the next goal while giving myself no comfort in completing the present goal, was not working for me. I always felt I had to complete the next article, book, workshop, etc. in order to feel good about myself. One day, I realized that I had it all wrong. My attempts to feel good about myself only after I had achieved created an extreme sense of urgency in me. If I allowed myself to feel worthy and whole before I started a goal, then I could still achieve things I wanted but without the excessive stress and pressure. It was a paradox to my linear thinking.

In the West, we are so focused on achievement that we base our identities and self-worth on the premise. If we less money than what we feel society approves of, or work at jobs that are not seen as valuable, we can feel that we are inadequate. Our desire to obtain the kind of life we want is

186

often clouded by the perceptions of what success is according to others. We are a success the moment we decide we want to live our lives with honor and integrity, not due to someone else's view of how much money we have, what position on the corporate ladder we are, or the type of crowd with whom we interact. We can enjoy the benefits of achievement, but if the only way we can love ourselves is through achievement, then we cannot find what it is we seek no matter what we achieve.

"And then he comes to that condition in late middle age: he's gotten to the top of the ladder, and found that it's against the wrong wall." – **Joseph Campbell**

On the flip side, examples of the negative qualities of fire can be seen in those people who rule the work place with an iron fist. These people react like a third world dictator since their mindset is on maintaining power rather than working together to achieve a desired outcome. In relationships this is the one who wants to control his or her partner through the use of intimidation, consistent criticism, and, in worst cases, violence. It can also manifest in the opposite manner as someone who gives up all power and does not direct his or her own life. This person will submit to everyone else's wishes and avoid taking any responsibility. The perceived lack of power will appear in the form of laziness, excessive submission to authority figures, and feelings of helplessness.

I remember working with a couple in a marriage counseling session which was a good example of the negative quality of fire in relationships. The couple, Al and Tiffany, had trouble connecting due to Tiffany's constant criticism of everything Al did. Tiffany felt so powerless in directing her own life that she unconsciously began directing Al's life. She criticized how much money he made, his job, his wardrobe, his friends, his enjoyment of reading, and many other aspects of his life. Al tried to not fight with Tiffany, but her daily assault based on her need to control her environment was just too much. She even criticized the way he brought her a blanket when he saw she was cold. It appeared that nothing Al did was right because, by allowing Al to be Al, Tiffany unconsciously felt she was giving up some of her power, which intensely frightened her.

Tiffany was unwilling to give Al any ground in their marital battles. In order to have a balanced fire element within the household, both parties needed to have some times where each could be right and other times when each could be wrong. The entire household was trying to adapt to Tiffany's excessive control and pressure, but it was weakening due to the unrelenting nature of unbalanced interactions. The couple eventually stopped therapy due to Tiffany's unyielding assertion that she was right about everything and that the whole problem was Al's inability to do things correctly (meaning Tiffany's way). I later heard they divorced. Al could take no more of his wife's controlling behavior.

The fire element corresponds with the work of Austrian psychiatrist, Alfred Adler. Adler was a psychoanalyst and a colleague of Sigmund Freud. He intensely studied how humans formed decisions about their lives based on their perceptions of superiority or inferiority. He believed that it was our feelings of inferiority that directed much of our behavior. Adler believed that our feelings of inferiority generally begin in childhood and continue to be present in our adult lives. These feelings occur when you perceive that another person has gained some form of power over you, criticizes you, or that someone is performing better than you think you can. Adler believed these feelings of inferiority are normal to all of us. He also believed if these feelings could motivate us to improve our lives, then they could be beneficial to us. If not properly used for motivation, then these feelings of inferiority can limit us. Those who believe they are powerless to change their inferior feelings often focus on the worst case scenarios for failure and convince themselves of their worthlessness. They avoid change and challenges since they are convinced they will fail.

Similarly, in Erik Erikson's psychosocial theory of emotional development, the decision to base who we are on what we accomplish is formed during a stage Erikson referred to as "industry versus inferiority." This stage happens between the ages of six and twelve. Children become able to perform more complex tasks as they enter the world of school. Children strive to master new ideas, concepts and skills. Those who receive encouragement and support by teachers and parents more frequently develop a confidence in

189

their ability to obtain a desired outcome. They have a belief in their new learnings and skills. For those children who receive no encouragement or are even harshly treated when they do not perform, they are more inclined to doubt their ability to be successful. If children do not believe they have achieved anything, even if it is outside the realm of academics, like sports or other hobbies, they may feel inferior to others. This may result in an unconscious belief that they are "not good enough", and they will make decisions based on feelings of self-doubt rather than on self-empowerment.

I could relate to this as I can today clearly remember when I was seven years old and in second grade. I had a teacher who was bordered on emotionally abusive in how she talked to her students. One never knew if she would lose her temper over some small matter. Her threshold for working with small children was minimal at best, and she seemed to take out her frustration on the students. One specific time stands out in my memory. We students were attempting to learn how to write cursive. She was getting frustrated that we were talking so long to complete, to her as an adult, a simple task. For most of us, we had never written in cursive before and were doing the best we could. She started yelling at us, "What is wrong with you people? Are just stupid or slow?" I remember her looking at me as she said these things, and in my child's brain, which uncritically takes in information from authority figures as gospel truth, I began to wonder if indeed I was smart enough or slow.

After that I approached school, which before interacting with this teacher had been a joyful experience, as if it were a place that reminded me that I was not good enough. From that point on my ability to learn things began to feel forced. It was almost as if there was a fog between me and the new material. I barely passed my studies and became very shy with most of my teachers. I barely made it out of high school (which I had to go to summer school to get an extra credit to get a diploma) and struggled in much of my undergraduate collegiate career. My unconscious mind had formed a limiting belief that I was not good enough, and when it came to academics, I must be slow. It was only when I reached graduate school that I was able to throw off the chains of academic self-doubt and started to thrive after I began to challenge my beliefs of not being good enough.

Exercise – Burning away the old

1. Remember a time when you first felt as if you were not good enough. Allow the emotions associated with that event come forth. Examine that situation from a third party perspective. Think about what resources the child version of you needed to be successful in that moment. Examine where you need those same resources in your life now.

2. Since a quality of fire is also to burn away unwanted things, build a small fire somewhere you can sit quietly and ponder the past condition you would now like to be different. Write down everything about that

old situation which has bothered you. List every emotion you felt and everything you experienced.

3. When you have completed your writing, fold the paper and sit quietly with your eyes closed. Allow yourself to become centered in your body. Say to yourself out loud, "I am now burning away this old situation and any old limiting beliefs and feelings which are tied to it."

4. Drop the paper in the fire and watch it burn, as it takes all the pain and hurt you used to feel with it. As the paper quickly changes form, realize that you too can quickly change form.

5. Write down how you would like to be in the future. Roll up this paper and put it in a very special place where you alone know where it resides.

6. Begin to notice small changes in how you react to old situations over the next three weeks. Write down the changes that you notice in your journal.

Fire meditation/visualization

The following visualization and meditation is designed to help connect you with the fire element at the unconscious level. Again, I recommend reading this part of the book into a recording device and playing it as you meditate on its subject matter. Go to a place where you know that you will not be disturbed and sit comfortably with your back straight. Take five very slow, long inhales and exhales of breath. Relax your jaw and become centered.

You imagine yourself sitting comfortably on the ground outdoors at night. You have built a fire for warmth and are enjoying the brilliant red and orange colors which emanate from it. You warm yourself in the glow of the fire. The heat of the fire makes you think of the heat of your own body and the energy being generated. This energy continues the beating of your heart and the functioning of your brain. The energy of the fire reminds you of the energy needed for chemical shifts in your body which create the proper functioning of our muscles. The energy which creates the pumping of blood in our hearts happens all by itself. You realize you do not have to force your heart to beat. You really allow yourself to let the warmth of the fire spread throughout your body. It feels so good to be warm and comfortable in this place. You begin to focus on your solar plexus area as you breathe in the wonderful warmth that is generated by the fire. As you exhale you imagine breathing out any old limitations which have previously held you back in some area of your life. It doesn't matter if these limitations are realistic or not as you let those emotions flow out of your body and into the fire in front of you. You begin to notice lightness in the body as you breathe in the energy of the fire and breathe out the former limitations you had. You continue to feel the comfortable warmth of the fire as you notice how different your body feels as it breathes in light and exhales out darkness. Your breathing has become a balanced process of bringing in good emotions and thoughts and getting rid of negativity and fear. After a little while, you begin to just sit comfortably as the star filled sky overhead shines down its energy and light upon you. You are amazed at the vastness of the universe and wonder how you were ever able to appear at this moment in time. The more you breathe in this fire energy, the more relaxed you become. You begin to notice how your body is very still, but feels so very alive as it connects with the wonder of the universe. You let your mind drift to think of new ideas and challenges you would like to enter into with the element of fire inside your mind. You wonder what differences you will see when you allow yourself to become alive with the energy of the fire element. A peace falls over you as you watch the fire quietly die down to beautiful embers as the sounds of nature around you continue to create their soothing symphony. You embrace the silence which follows as you allow yourself to drift off into a deeper feeling of relaxation.

CHAPTER 9: AIR

The element of Air has been viewed as a manifestation of emotion and intelligence. Inspiration and intellect are hallmarks of this element. The creation of new ideas, perceptions and acquiring knowledge originate in the air element. Traditionally, air represented the direction of East and the season of spring. Air has also been seen as the realm of peace and interconnection. Balance in this area appears as compassion, understanding and consideration of other people. Interactions with others are focused on harmony and connection instead of conflict and separation. The intellect is utilized to create synergistic outcomes that benefit all parties involved.

By allowing our hearts and our minds to work together, we can create an environment of understanding and empathy for our fellow human beings while still achieving our dreams and goals. In balancing the energy of this element we will find it easier to work with others for common intentions and to allow others to follow their own directives for their lives. We begin to allow more spontaneity and imagination into our interactions as we are less driven by a strict idea of what is to happen in our lives. We can accept our faults and the faults of others more gracefully as we realize that everyone is doing the best they can with what they have and where they are now.

In this element we blend our intellect and our feelings to increase our emotional intelligence. Emotional intelligence is our ability to observe our own, as well as others', emotions and to use this information to direct our thinking and actions. The ability to observe our emotion and to process the observed information has been found to play an important part in our ability to regulate our emotions. Emotional intelligence allows us to effectively use our emotions to think more clearly and become more self-aware and empathic. When we are balanced in our emotional states and approach others with empathy we find that we naturally grow happier and more accepting of how the world really is.

When we are unbalanced in this element on one side, we may find ourselves overly sympathetic to others which can result in our being manipulated by those who prey upon our emotional weaknesses. Sometimes we feel guilt ridden with a heavy sense of obligation to others in spite of no apparent reason for feeling so. On the other hand, if we are unbalanced at this element we may find that we are lacking in empathy and kindness and appear to be someone who has no heart. We may have a drive to succeed and will move forward toward our goal while bulldozing over others.

As we move into this element, we are now challenged to begin allowing other people to be the way they are without our trying to control them. We are challenged to accept people as they are and love them in spite of what they do. We have to let go and allow the world to be as it is. We will not be attached to outcomes as strongly as we may have been in the past. When we realize that the world is a projection of ourselves, we can see that there is nothing to change other than ourselves. We realize that we are who we are, and in the

196

moment, we have a choice to change or to continue as we are. In order to do this, we have to use both our intellects and our hearts to accept ourselves as we are.

This is very difficult for many of us because we feel the need to constantly improve and adjust ourselves since we are not good enough. When we rationally look at how we feel, we are always attached to some ideal of how we are "supposed" to be. This is rooted in a narcissism which keeps us from connecting with others. We become so self-focused on what we "should" be that we miss the importance of what we "are." We often judge our worth by our behaviors rather than by our being. When we allow ourselves to feel worth and acceptance just because we are alive and human, we give ourselves the ability to have more choices as to what actions we take in life. It is a paradox that the more we accept our faults, the easier it is to change them. Damning ourselves (and others) for our behaviors only creates a vicious cycle of self-condemnation which replays the very action for which we condemned ourselves.

Psychologist Carl Rogers believed that the root of many of our problems arises due to our inability to give ourselves what he referred to as, unconditional positive regard. This is when we love and accept ourselves for what we are rather than what we do. Rogers believed that the more unconditional positive regard that we can give ourselves, the more we are willing to adjust and try new actions even if we make mistakes. This requires us to suspend any judgment about ourselves, accept what is, and decide without guilt or shame, what it is we want to do in the future.

When we are balanced in the air element, we can also begin caring for others in a manner that is not contaminated by our judgment. We find that we can give others unconditional positive regard without being overly critical of how they are living their lives. We give because we want to help, not because we want to be in charge of other people. We see both the strengths and faults in everyone, but we do not harshly judge since we realize that we, too, are capable of anything that any other person has done or will do.

The primary goal in this element is to get our own weak ego out of the way. This is one of the most challenging things a person can attempt since our ego can rule with an iron fist. I define "ego" as our sense of self. If we have a strong sense of self, we realize that we do not have to prove anything to anyone. We focus our energy on doing the things which are important to us and bring us joy. We help others because we feel it is the right thing to do. We accept where we are in the moment knowing we can change things if so desired.

If we do not have a strong sense of self, we often become overly competitive with others and judge them harshly as, unconsciously, we view ourselves as unworthy, and we project these feelings onto others. We feel that we have to constantly justify our actions to others and to seek their approval for our dreams and goals in life. We may become contentious and overly judgmental while waving the "moral flag" but down deep we do not really believe we are acceptable, moral people. We think we are never good enough and can never be good enough. This can result in our controlling others who have not performed to our standards.

Our ego constantly tells us that we have to defend ourselves for our beliefs. We feel we have to justify ourselves to everyone. This can create further anxiety for us as we constantly rush to let others know why we take certain actions and build a case to win their approval. Our ego also wants to take credit for things we do in order to gain acceptance of others. We may feel we have to let everyone know how kind, generous and compassionate we are when we do nice things for others. Our ego searches for the spotlight. I remember hearing a group of ladies at a health food store get into a spat about which one of them recycled the most as this proved who was a more spiritual person. By not defending ourselves or feel we have to take credit we release the tight constraint our ego imposes on us.

Exercise - Pay attention to judgments

Spend today noticing how quickly you rush to judgments about other people. Pay attention to your thoughts about others and how you instantly label them in your mind. As soon as you notice your habitual way of rushing to judgment, ask what other ways you could think about the person. Before you criticize anyone's actions, ask yourself when you have done something similar. The more you find yourself judging others, the more you can accept others' faults.

Exercise - Helping without recognition

Find a cause that you feel is very important and anonymously donate to the cause. Tell no one about your donation. Begin to notice how a part of you wants to let others know how "generous" you are. Accept that a part of you wants approval of your generosity, but resist the urge to spread the news that you are helping others. The ego will want to inform everyone you know of the good deeds we have done so that we can feel validated and worthy. When we have mastered the air element we no longer need to seek approval for our goodness, without any fanfare we can be content with feeling good about our actions.

Air meditation/visualization

The following visualization and meditation is designed to help connect you with the air element at the unconscious level. Again, I recommend reading this part of the book into a recording device and playing it as you meditate on its subject matter. Go to a place where you know you won't be disturbed and sit comfortably with your back straight. Take five very slow, long inhales and exhales of breath. Relax your jaw and become centered.

Settle yourself in a comfortable position and allow your mind to relax. Become aware of your breathing. Notice the patterns of inhaling and exhaling. Imagine yourself sitting comfortably high above on a hill where you alone are taking in the view. You watch the clouds glide across the sky and see the trees sway in the wind. You even notice the grass move in the comfortable breeze. You are very still and comfortable as you breathe in fresh, clean air. You notice the rhythmic qualities of your breath. It flows in and out of your lungs as your eyes scan far and wide from your high vantage point. You recognize that the air surrounding you and touching your skin is the same air which moves the clouds along in the horizon and moves the branches of the trees in the distance. As the element of air comes inside your body, it dissolves in your bloodstream to be used for energy to aid in your health and wellness. You feel no divide between the air that is outside yourself and the air inside yourself. We notice that we can never hold onto air for too long as our lungs will automatically push out the old air to make way for the new air. We can only use it and then let it go. It is the same air that everyone uses. You reflect that every person has to use the same air, and that air does not discriminate in whom it enters and exits. We don't own the air, we only use it. You recognize that every person needs air and no matter what he or she has done or will do, the need for air is constant. As you continue to slowly and comfortably breathe in and out the wonderful gift of fresh, clean air, you find that you begin to feel a sense of wonder about the world. You reflect on how everything needs the air as you do. You realize that there is little difference between yourself and others in this aspect of existence. The air that has come into and out of your lungs has now gone out into the world where it is being used by everything else. You breathe more deeply and as you reflect upon the notion that all that is outside you has been inside you as well. You feel a connection to all things and all people when you focus on your breath. You continue to watch the trees and grass gently sway in the cool but comfortable breeze.

The more you relax and breathe in this wonderful air, the more you can become aware of the place in your life where you can begin to accept total responsibility for your choices. You find that you can let things go from the past as you embrace the present moment of breathing deeply. As you have nothing to prove to anyone, you can become more open to new experiences. You enjoy the present moment and envision a compelling future where you will become even more creative. You know that you can begin to live your life far beyond the pull of material gains. Breathing in and out the wonderful element of air can remind you that you are deeply connected to everyone and everything. Being yourself becomes easier as your ego's desires recede and your compassion toward others increases.

You scan over the horizon and enjoy the perfect view of the landscape which evokes a feeling of awe in you as your awareness expands. Taking in the incredible views and feeling the wonderful breeze on your skin, you can really let go of all expectations of the next moment and become more open to the present moment. As the sun shines down on you, you have a feeling of gratitude for being able to experience this moment. Any need to be something other than you are now disappears. Life is perfect as it is in this one moment. You close your eyes and hear the sounds of landscape operate in perfect harmony. All is as it should be.

EPILOGUE: A MAGICAL LIFE

After I spent a year exploring the world from a magical perspective, I find that I enjoy being alive much more. I still have good days and bad days, but overall I embrace and love the simple fact that I exist. I now know that my being alive is not merely an accident. I am part of a vast interconnected system that moves forward at its own pace and on its own time. I am just as important in this system as my next door neighbor, the birds that fly over my home, and the trees in my backyard. I have become more mindful of my actions since they directly have consequences on the world that I inhabit. Even though I had previously understood this idea on an intellectual level, the actual experience of living magically has given me a real sense of this interconnection. I now have a deep feeling of sacredness toward the world around me, which previously had been merely a cerebral exercise.

I also find that I have been able to let go of a great deal of emotional baggage that I had been carrying with me. By experiencing that I am part of something greater than myself, I have been able to shift my perspective about my life. I am beginning to work toward acceptance of what "is" and forgiveness toward those who have disappointed me in the past. I now see that each person has his or her own path to walk in life. In order for this wonderful interconnected system to work effectively; each person needs to find his or her own way. Letting go and allowing the natural flow of life really is the secret to happiness.

This world is a gloriously beautiful and mysterious place. The more we investigate it, the more surprised we are in what we find. By acknowledging that we are all part of this beauty and mystery, we find that there are no real barriers between us. We are all much more alike than not. We are all needed to make this system function. By realizing that each of us is a necessary component of this wondrous experience, maybe we can begin to treat each other with more kindness, compassion and love. Life can truly be magical, if we allow it.